THE BELI

and

PRACTICES

OF JUDAISM

By LOUIS FINKELSTEIN

PRESIDENT, JEWISH THEOLOGICAL SEMINARY
OF AMERICA

THE DEVIN-ADAIR COMPANY

NEW YORK

1945

CONTENTS

BIBLIOGRAPHY   vi

I—INTRODUCTION   3

II—THE PLACE OF STUDY IN JUDAISM   10

III—THE PLACE OF ETHICS IN JUDAISM   15

IV—THE BASIC CONCEPTS OF JUDAISM   20

V—THE SYSTEM OF BLESSINGS   36

VI—THE SYNAGOGUE AND THE PRAYERS   39

VII—THE SABBATH AND THE FESTIVALS   50

VIII—SPECIAL OCCASIONS IN THE COURSE OF LIFE   74

IX—THE JEWISH HOME AND THE DIETARY LAWS   84

X—THE JEWISH HOPE FOR THE FUTURE   89

INDEX   91

BIBLIOGRAPHY

Judaism, I. Epstein, London, 1939.
The Jewish Religion, Michael Friedlaender, New York, 1923.
Laws and Customs, Gerald Friedlander, London, 1921.
The Jewish Religion, Julius Greenstone, Philadelphia, 1920.
Judaism as Creed and Life, Morris Joseph, London, 1903.
The Meaning of Modern Jewish Religion, M. M. Kaplan, New York, 1937.
Reform Movement in Judaism, David Philipson, New York, 1931.

I. INTRODUCTION

JUDAISM is a way of life which endeavors to transform virtually every human action into a means of communion with God. Through this communion with God, the Jew is enabled to make his contribution to the establishment of the Kingdom of God and the brotherhood of men on earth. So far as its adherents are concerned, Judaism seeks to extend the concept of right and wrong to every aspect of their behavior. Jewish rules of conduct apply not merely to worship, ceremonial, and justice between man and man, but also to such matters as philanthropy, personal friendships and kindnesses, intellectual pursuits, artistic creation, courtesy, the preservation of health, and the care of diet.[1]

So rigorous is this discipline, as ideally conceived in Jewish writings, that it may be compared to those specified for members of religious orders in other faiths. A casual conversation or a thoughtless remark may, for instance, be considered a grave violation of Jewish Law. It is forbidden, not merely as a matter of good form, but of religious law, to use obscene language, to rouse a person to anger, or to display unusual ability in the presence of the handicapped. The ceremonial observances are equally detailed. The ceremonial Law expects that each Jew will pray

[1] Without desiring to ascribe to them any responsibility for this paper, I record with deep gratitude the assistance in its preparation given by colleagues from different schools of Jewish thought. These include Rabbis Max Arzt, Ben Zion Bokser, Samuel S. Cohon, Judah Goldin, Israel M. Goldman, Simon Greenberg, David de Sola Pool, Samuel Schulman, and Aaron J. Tofield.

thrice every day, if possible at the synagogue; to recite a blessing before and after each meal; to thank God for any special pleasure, such as a curious sight, the perfume of a flower, or the receipt of good news, wear a fringed garment about his body; to recite certain passages from Scripture each day; and to don *tephillin* (cubical receptacles containing certain Biblical passages) during the morning prayers.

The decisions regarding right and wrong under given conditions are not left for the moment, but are formulated with great care in the vast literature created by the Jewish religious teachers. At the heart of this literature are the Hebrew Scriptures, usually described as the Old Testament, consisting of the Five Books of Moses (usually called the *Torah*), the Prophets, and the Hagiographa. These works, particularly the Five Books of Moses, contain the prescriptions for human conduct composed under Divine inspiration. The ultimate purpose of Jewish religious study is the application of the principles enunciated in the Scriptures, to cases and circumstances which the principles do not explicitly cover.

Because Judaism is a way of life, no confession of faith can by itself make one a Jew. Belief in the dogmas of Judaism must be expressed in the acceptance of its discipline, rather than in the repetition of a verbal formula. But no failure either to accept the beliefs of Judaism or to follow its prescriptions is sufficient to exclude from the fold a member of the Jewish faith. According to Jewish tradition, the covenant between God and Moses on Mount Sinai included all those who were present and also all of their descendants. This covenant was reaffirmed in the days of Ezra and Nehemiah, when the people together with their leaders made "a sure covenant to walk in God's law, which was given to Moses the servant of God, and to observe and do all the commandments of the Lord our Lord, and His ordinances and His statutes" (Nehemiah 10.30). To apply the words used by Scripture in another connection, this covenant has thus been made binding upon the Jews, "and upon their seed, and upon all such as joined themselves unto them" (Esther 9.27). There is therefore no need for any ceremony to admit a Jewish child into the faith of Judaism. Born in a Jewish household, he becomes at once "a child of the covenant." The fact that the child has Jewish parents involves the assumption of the obligations which God has placed on these parents and their descendants.

This concept of the inheritance of religious traditions does not imply any sense of racial differentiation. The concept derives simply from the belief that a person may assume binding obligations not only for himself, but also for his descendants. Thus anyone who is converted to Judaism assumes the obligation to observe its discipline, and makes this obligation binding on his descendants forever, precisely as if he had been an Israelite, standing with Moses, before Mount Sinai on the day of the Revelation.

The ancestry of the proselyte and therefore his "race," are quite irrelevant matters. Whether he be of Arabic background, like Queen Helene, or Roman, like Aquila, or Chazar, like the members of the south Russian kingdom which became converted to Judaism in the eighth century of the Christian era, or Norman like Obadiah, the well known Crusader who became a proselyte, or Polish, like the famous Count Valentine Potocki of the eighteenth century, his descendants, from the point of view of Judaism, would all be bound by his obligation to follow the laws and customs of Judaism.

On the other hand, in view of the Jewish attitude to other monotheistic faiths, it is considered improper for a Jew to urge a member of another faith to become a Jew. Indeed, a person who desires to adopt Judaism must be told of all the difficulties which are inherent in affiliation with the faith. Only a person who persists in his desire to become a Jew, and demonstrates that his desire is based on no mundane motive, may be accepted into the Jewish fold.

Because of the special place which the home occupies in Judaism as a center of religious life and worship, almost coordinate with the synagogue itself, Judaism holds it essential that both parties to a Jewish marriage be members of the Jewish faith. There is, of course, no objection to marriage with a sincere convert to Judaism. But it is not possible for the home to function in the manner prescribed by Jewish law unless both husband and wife are of the Jewish faith.

In the case of a mixed marriage, the status of the children is determined by the faith of the mother, as the greatest influence in their lives. The children of a Christian mother are considered Christians; the children of a Jewish mother are considered Jews. The Jewish partner in such a mixed marriage is considered living in continual transgression of Jewish law, but remains, like those who deviate from the Law in other respects, within the fold of Judaism, entirely subject to the duties and obligations placed on other Jews.

While no one outside of the Jewish faith is bound by the rules of Jewish ceremonial discipline, Judaism draws a distinction between the adherents of monotheistic faiths, including Christianity and Islam, which are recognized as making a distinctive contribution to the realization of the Kingdom of God on earth, and non-monotheistic faiths. The various regulations which Judaism, like early Christianity, established to prevent reversion to paganism, obviously have no application to the relationship between Jews and their neighbors in Christian and Mohammedan countries. A Jew may not enter a building dedicated to idol-worship even to protect himself from inclement weather; and of course, he cannot participate in any festivity dedicated to any form of idol-worship.

These ceremonial rules are intended to register a protest against paganism; they do not place the pagan in any inferior position with regard to Jewish law or ethic. According to Philo and Josephus, it is a violation of Jewish law for a Jew to speak with disrespect of the gods of any people, for the verse, "Thou shalt not revile God" (Exodus 22.27), is interpreted as applying to all gods. While this interpretation is not accepted in the rabbinic tradition, it does express the spirit with which Judaism approaches all systems of belief, regardless of the extent of their difference from itself.

This spirit is expressed in the principle that every rule of moral conduct which a Jew must observe toward another Jew applies also to relations with persons of other faiths. The laws of justice, kindness, and charity, as well as the obligation to visit the sick, bury the dead, support the needy, must be assumed for all people.

Like other religions, Judaism can be, and indeed has been practiced under various forms of civil government: monarchical, semi-monarchical, feudal, democratic, and totalitarian. The members of the Jewish faith, like those of other religions, regard themselves as citizens or subjects of their respective states. In all synagogues prayers are offered for the safety of the government of the country;

and in the ancient Temple of Jerusalem daily sacrifices were offered on behalf of the Imperial Roman Government, as long as Palestine remained under its dominion. This patriotic loyalty to the state has often persisted in the face of cruel persecution. The principle followed has been that formulated by the ancient teacher, Rabbi Haninah, "Pray for the welfare of the government; for without fear of the government, men would have swallowed each other up alive."

Despite this ability to adjust itself to the exigencies of any form of temporal government, Judaism, like other faiths derived from the Prophets, has always upheld the principles of the Fatherhood of God and the dignity and worth of Man as the child and creature of God; and its ideals are more consistent with those of democracy than any other system of government.

The most vigorous and consistent effort to formulate the discipline of Judaism in terms of daily life was that made in ancient Palestine and Babylonia. The Palestinian schools devoted to this purpose were founded in the second century before the Christian era, and flourished in their original form for six centuries and in a somewhat altered form until the Crusades. The Babylonian schools were founded in the third century of the Christian era, and ended the first and most significant phase of their activity about three hundred years later.

The rules of conduct worked out in the discussions of these academies form the substance of Jewish Law. In arriving at these precepts, the ancient teachers were guided by their desire to know the will of God. So far as possible they sought to discover His will through an intensive study of the Scriptures. Where Scripture offered no clear guidance they tried to ascertain His will by applying its general principle of moral right. In addition, they had a number of oral traditions, going back to antiquity, which they regarded as supplementary to the written Law, and equal to it in authority and inspiration.

The high purpose of the discussions made them of monumental importance to Judaism. As a result, they were committed to memory by eager and faithful disciples, until the memorized material grew to such proportions that it had to be reduced to writing. The work in which the discussions were thus preserved is known as the Talmud. As there were two groups of academies, differing slightly from one another in their interpretation of the Law, and widely in their manner of approach to the subject, we have two Talmudim, that of Palestine and that of Babylonia. Both are considered authoritative guides for Jewish Law. Where they disagree, the Babylonian Talmud is, for historical reasons, considered the more authoritative.

II. THE PLACE OF STUDY IN JUDAISM

It is quite impossible to understand Judaism without an appreciation of the place which it assigns to the study and practice of the Talmudic Law. Doing the will of God is the primary spiritual concern of the Jew. Therefore, to this day, he must devote considerable time not merely to the mastery of the content of the Talmud, but also to training in its method of reasoning. The study of the Bible and the Talmud is thus far more than a pleasing intellectual exercise, and is itself a means of communion with God. According to some teachers, this study is the highest form of such communion imaginable.[2]

Because the preservation of the Divine will regarding human conduct is basic to all civilization, none of the commandments is more important than that of studying and teaching the Law. The most sacred object in Judaism is the scroll containing the Five Books of Moses. Every synagogue must contain at least one copy of it. The scroll must be placed in a separate Ark, before which burns the eternal light. The position of this Ark in the synagogue is in the direction of Jerusalem; everyone turns toward the Ark in prayer. When the scroll is taken from the Ark for the purpose of reading, all those present must rise. No irreverent or profane action may be performed in a room which contains a scroll, nor may a scroll be moved from place to place except for the performance of religious rites. From

[2] See the essay on "Study as a Mode of Worship," by Professor Nathan Isaacs, in *The Jewish Library*, edited by Rabbi Leo Jung, 1928, pp. 51-70.

time to time the scroll must be examined to ascertain that its writing is intact.

The preparation of the scroll is a task requiring much care, erudition, and labor. It is usually done by a professional copyist called a *sofer* (scribe). The text is written on sheets of parchment, especially prepared for the purpose. Only skins of animals permitted for food, in accordance with Leviticus 11.1-9 and Deuteronomy 14.3-9, are used. The whole work is then attached at the beginning and at the end to wooden rods, so that it can be rolled in the form of a scroll.

The ink used in writing must be black, and should be indelible. Before beginning to copy the text, the scribe must say, "I am about to write this book as a sacred scroll of the Law." He repeats a similar formula every time he is about to copy the Divine Name, saying, "I am writing this word as the sacred Name."

Like other Semitic languages, Hebrew requires only a consonantal text for reading: the vowels are omitted in classical texts. Hence the scroll of the Five Books of Moses contains only the consonantal text. This text is fixed by tradition, almost to the last detail. Even such matters as division into paragraphs and sections, and the special size of certain letters, which are particularly large or particularly small, is determined. The texts of all the extant scrolls are thus virtually identical. Any significant deviation from the traditional text makes a scroll unfit for use, and must be corrected as soon as it is discovered. No decorations or illuminations are permitted in the scrolls intended for the public service. Tradition prescribes, however, that certain poetic portions are to be written in verse form, and that certain letters shall have little coronets adorning them.

No less important than this homage paid to the scroll as symbol of the Law, is that paid to the living Law itself. Fully three-fourths of the Hebrew literature produced within the first nineteen centuries of the Christian era, is devoted to the elucidation of the Law. The best minds in Judaism have been devoted to its study. Every parent is required to teach his child its basic elements. Its study is considered vital not only for the guidance it offers in the practice of Judaism, but for liberation from the burden of secular ambition and anxieties. The study of the Law is believed to be a foretaste of the immortal life, for the sages of the Talmud believed that Paradise itself could offer men no nearer communion with God than the opportunity of discovering His will in the study of the Law.

The Talmud derives its authority from the position held by the ancient academies. The teachers of these academies, both those of Babylonia and of Palestine, were considered the rightful successors of the older *Sanhedrin* or Supreme Court, which before the destruction of Jerusalem (in the year 70 of the Christian era) was the arbiter of Jewish Law and custom. The Sanhedrin derived its authority from the statement in Deuteronomy 17.8-13, that whenever a question of interpretation of the Law arises, it is to be finally decided by the sages and priests in Jerusalem.

At the present time, the Jewish people have no living central authority comparable in status to the ancient Sanhedrin or the later academies. Therefore any decision regarding Jewish religion must be based on the Talmud, as the final résumé of the teachings of those authorities when they existed. The right of an individual to decide questions of religious Law depends entirely on his knowledge of the Bible, the Talmud, and the later manuals based on them, and upon his fidelity to their teachings. Those who have acquired this knowledge are called rabbis. There is no sharp distinction in religious status between the rabbi and the layman in Judaism. The rabbi is simply a layman especially learned in Scripture and Talmud. Nor is there any hierarchical organization or government among the rabbis of the world. Yet some rabbis, by virtue of their especial distinction in learning, by common consent come to be regarded as superior authorities on questions of Jewish Law. Difficult and complicated issues are referred to them for clarification.

To be recognized as a rabbi, a Talmudic student customarily is ordained. Traditionally, the authority to act as rabbi may be conferred by any other rabbi. It is usual, however, for students at various theological schools to receive this authority from their teachers. In America, there are several rabbinical schools, each of which ordains its graduates in the manner in which degrees are conferred on graduates of other institutions of learning. At present (1941) the best known of these schools are as follows:

Hebrew Theological College, Chicago
Hebrew Union College, Cincinnati
Jewish Institute of Religion, New York City
Jewish Theological Seminary of America, New York City
Rabbi Isaac Elchanan Theological Seminary, New York City

There is considerable variation among the interpretations of Judaism taught at these seminaries, and consequently there is a considerable difference in emphasis on the subjects included in their respective curricula. This has resulted from the fact that during the past century various groups of rabbis, primarily in Germany and America, have claimed authority not merely to interpret, but also to amend Talmudic, and even Biblical Law. These rabbis are known as reform rabbis, and their congregations as reform congregations. Of the rabbis who adhere to traditional Judaism, some reject any significant innovations from customary practice; these rabbis are called orthodox. Others maintain that Jewish law is a living tradition, subject to change, but they insist that such changes must be made in accordance with traditional canons for the interpretation and development of rabbinic law. These rabbis are usually called "conservative."

The differences between the various groups of American rabbis have not led to any sectarian schism. Although the difference in practice between the traditional and reform groups is considerable, each accepts the other as being within the fold of Judaism. It is possible for them to do so, because of the principle that even an unobservant or a heretical Jew does not cease to be a member of the covenant made between God and Israel at the time of the Revelation. Only actual rejection of Judaism, by affiliation with another faith, is recognized as separating one from the Jewish community.[3] So long as a member of the Jewish faith has not by overt act or word and of his own free will declared himself a member of another religion, other Jews are bound to regard him as one of their own faith, and to seek his return to its practice and beliefs.

[3] The extent to which even conversion to another faith affects the status of an individual within Judaism, is a subject of considerable discussion in rabbinical literature. Many authorities consider such a person a Jew, despite his conversion. The prevailing opinion, however, recognizes as effective the voluntary separation of a person from Judaism.

III. THE PLACE OF ETHICS IN JUDAISM

The ceremonial discipline is considered obligatory only on members of the Jewish faith, but the ethical element in Judaism is universal in scope. The commandment against murder is explicitly stated in Scripture to have been revealed to Noah (Genesis 9.5); and therefore applies to all humankind. By analogy, the commandments against theft, cruelty to animals, sexual license, blasphemy, idol-worship, and the violation of civil justice, are considered to be universal. Those who observe these fundamental laws are considered "the righteous of the peoples of the world," who will partake in the resurrection and in im-mortality.

One further distinction is made between the ethical and ceremonial content of Judaism. When faced with the danger of death, one may violate any of the commandments, save only those against murder, sexual license, and idolatry. This rule does not apply in the event of a religious persecution. When a government undertakes to suppress the observance of Judaism, it becomes the duty of the Jew to submit to martyrdom rather than deviate from his faith, in even a slight matter.

The duty of accepting martyrdom, either for the ethical Law in the normal course of events, or for the whole of the Law in times of persecution, is called *Kiddush ha-Shem*, (sanctification of the Name of God). Any violation of this duty is called the profanation of the Name of God, *Hillul ha-Shem*. These terms may also be applied to situations which do not call for martyrdom, but where it is possible to increase or lessen respect for religious faith through action. Anyone who through sacrifice and saintliness brings others to more profound recognition of God, "sanctifies" the Name of God. But anyone whose actions bring religion generally and Judaism in particular into disrespect, is guilty of *Hillul ha-Shem*. Because of this principle, religious leaders are expected to be particularly careful of their ethical conduct, for even the slightest deviation from propriety on their part naturally casts aspersion on the whole faith. Similarly, any impropriety on the part of a Jew in his relations with members of other faiths tends to decrease respect for Judaism as a faith, and is therefore "a profanation of the Name of God."

The application of the ethical teachings of Judaism to every aspect of daily life has necessarily involved the creation and development of a system of civil law. Like contemporary Christians, the Jews of the Talmudic period believed it wrong to resort to the pagan courts of their time for adjudication of civil differences. Not only did the Jewish conception of justice frequently differ from that of the pagans, but the pagan courts were often corrupt, and almost always cruel. The tradition opposing the use of civil courts for adjudication of civil disputes, persisted during the Middle Ages. For many centuries secular courts were few and inaccessible, and even in later periods their judgments were generally considered unfair. Only with the enlightenment of the eighteenth and nineteenth centuries, and the disappearance of the ghettos, have Jews become accustomed to apply to secular courts of justice for settlement of their litigation. However, it is a fundamental principle of Talmudic Law that the civil law of a country is binding, and a Jewish court would necessarily have to take cognizance of the civil law on any disputed point.

The necessity of dealing with civil litigation compelled the Talmudic sages and their mediaeval successors to give much attention to this aspect of the Jewish law. Hence, about one-fourth of the Babylonian Talmud, and a proportionate share of later rabbinic literature, is devoted to questions of civil law. The latest compilation of this law is to be found in the *Hoshen Mishpat*, the fourth volume of Rabbi Joseph Caro's famous code, the *Shulhan Aruk*.

The Jewish civil law is frequently applied even today in the adjudication of disputes arising among religious functionaries, and is sometimes used as a basis for arbitration agreements.

But the Jewish conception of justice transcends the realm of civil law. Justice includes all ethical conduct, as well as philanthropy. Indeed, the word for charity in rabbinic Hebrew is *sedakah*, or righteousness. Under certain circumstances, Talmudic law actually permits courts to compel a man to do his duty by the community or by individuals, beyond the letter of the law.

As a rule, a Jew is expected to give between one-tenth and one-fifth of his income to charitable purposes. To give less than one-tenth is to fail in duty to the community; to give more than a fifth may involve injustice to the immediate family. Beyond provision of material assistance for the needy and suffering, lies the duty of encouraging them with personal attention and kind words, of recognizing them as personal friends, and above all enabling them to help themselves. In his Code, Maimonides recognizes eight types of philanthropy, arranged according to their merit, as follows: 1) helping the needy to be self-dependent by providing opportunity for work; 2) giving charity to the poor in such a way that neither the donor nor the recipient know one another; 3) giving charity in such a way that the donor can identify the recipient but the recipient cannot identify the donor; 4) giving in such a way that the recipient can identify the donor but the donor cannot identify the recipient; 5) giving in such a way that the donor and recipient know each other, provided the gift is made before it is requested; 6) giving after a request is made, provided the amount is sufficient to meet the need; 7) giving less than is needed, but with a kindly countenance; 8) giving less than is needed, and without a kindly countenance.

Judaism lays great stress on the importance of personal ethical relations between friends. The last of the Ten Commandments is a prohibition against "coveting" the blessings of a neighbor. Other regulations warn against talebearing, gossip, envy, and dislike of a neighbor. Any form of vengeance is also prohibited. If a person says to another, "Lend me your hatchet," and the second reply, "I will not lend you my hatchet today, because yesterday you refused to lend me your sickle," the second transgresses the commandment, "Thou shalt not take vengeance" (Leviticus 19.18). If the second reply, "I will lend you my hatchet, despite the fact that yesterday you refused to lend me your sickle," he transgresses the second half of the verse, "nor bear any grudge." The importance of these commandments in Judaism is such that one of the most distinguished Jewish scholars of the eleventh century, Bahya ibn Pakuda, devoted a whole book to their analysis, the *Book of the Duties of the Heart*. In our own generation, the famous Rabbi Israel Meir Kahan (better known by the title of his book, *Chofetz Chayyim,* first published anonymously) devoted his life to warning against the transgression of these laws of ethical conduct. During the nineteenth century, there developed under the influence of Rabbi Israel Salanter (d. 1883) a whole group of students who refrained from conversation over long periods, in order to discipline themselves against the sin of "evil speech."

In accordance with the precept of Leviticus 19.17, Judaism considers every member of the faith responsible for the moral conduct of those neighbors over whom he is able to exert helpful influence. To see injustice done without protesting against it, is to participate in the injustice. To provoke a man to anger, is to partake of the sin of unjust anger. To permit an opposing litigant to take a false oath, is to share in the transgression of perjury; just as to listen to blasphemy, gossip, or talebearing is to be a party to them. The concept is summarized in the teaching of Rabbi Jacob that "a person, on whose account God has to inflict punishment on another, will not be admitted into the presence of God" (*Shabbat* 149b). The underlying principle of this teaching is the doctrine that a victim of injustice falls short of the ideal of Judaism to the extent that he fails to obtain Divine forgiveness for the person who acted unjustly toward him.

The public confession of sins prescribed for the Day of Atonement (see below) reflects this consciousness that every member of the community is to some extent responsible for the sins of every other member. The confession lists not only the sins which the average man is liable to commit through oversight, but also such sins as theft, unchastity, rendering false judgment, which are obviously not committed with the vast majority.

IV. THE BASIC CONCEPTS OF JUDAISM

The central doctrine of Judaism is the belief in the One God, the Father of all mankind. The first Hebrew words which a Jewish child learns are the confession of faith contained in the verse, "Hear, O Israel, the Lord is our God, the Lord is One," and every believing Jew hopes that as he approaches his end in the fulness of time, he will be sufficiently conscious to repeat this same confession. This monotheistic belief is subject to no qualification or compromise.

Another doctrine, which has become universal in Judaism, is the belief in the incorporeality of God, i.e., the belief that God has no physical, visible form.

A third doctrine, equally important, is the timelessness and omnipresence of God. As one of the Talmudic sages states, "God is the place of the Universe; the Universe cannot be regarded as His place."

While these concepts seem to put God far beyond the reach of even the most speculative human thought and imagination, Judaism insists also on God's accessibility to every human being who seeks Him. Every person may pray to Him, and His providence surrounds every phenomenon of human life. One of the great Palestinian sages of the third century of the Christian era, expressed this paradox in the following words: "Wherever Scripture describes the greatness of God, it also insists on His humility."

It is an error, however, according to Jewish theology to attribute to God even those good qualities which are found in man. To speak of God as being merciful in the sense in which man is merciful, is almost blasphemy, for in human life, mercy must sometimes be a mitigation of justice, and require a departure from courses dictated by wisdom and prudence. Such a deviation from justice or wisdom is necessitated by man's limited knowledge and vision, and the consequent necessity of distrusting his reason. In infinite wisdom and knowledge, justice and mercy necessarily become 'identical. When we speak of God as merciful, or kind, or loving, we do so in order to give expression to our human conceptions of Him. The manner of speech resembles in a way our necessarily partial and inadequate descriptions of physical phenomena. Yet just as descriptions of the physical universe, inadequate as they are, help us understand it, so our use of attributes enables us, to some extent at least, to appreciate God's ways with man.

It is a cardinal principle of Judaism that the highest form of piety is to perform the will of God out of love for Him, rather than out of fear of Him. To develop love for God, and to do His will, without any thought of the punishments He may inflict or the rewards He may offer, is one of the most difficult of disciplines. Many rabbini-sages endured personal affliction without murmur, but suffered anguish at the frustration of God's will in the world through human sin and waywardness.

While Judaism does not consider fear of punishment the principal reason for submission to Divine will, it recognizes the fact that disobedience necessarily entails suffering. This is not due to the fact that God, like an angry human parent or ruler, penalizes those who transgress His will. It is, rather, because the Divine discipline, as incorporated in Jewish tradition, is directed toward giving man as much happiness as can be obtained in life. Failure to conduct oneself in accordance with this discipline has the same effect on man's happiness, that failure to observe the rules of hygiene has on man's health. When we say that God punishes those who transgress His will, we mean that wicked actions inevitably deprive men of the happiness which would be in store for them if they followed the dictates of religion and ethics.

Because of God's love for men, He has made it possible for them to escape some of the consequences of error and sinful conduct. Most errors can be rectified through true repentance. Indeed, repentance sometimes makes it possible for the experience of error itself to become a virtue. The fact that a person has not lived in accordance with the discipline of religion does not, therefore, condemn him to suffering. It merely places on him the obligation to repent of his error, and return to God. He will find that in this return to God, he obtains the same measure of happiness awarded to those who have never committed a transgression.

However, repentance cannot always be achieved. If a man injures his neighbor, he will not be able to repent completely, or win peace of mind, until he has won the forgiveness of his neighbor. Rulers, who mislead their people, causing whole nations and races to indulge in wrong-doing, and to that extent deflecting the development of human civilization, cannot repent. They may be willing to rectify their wrong; but the power to rectify it will be beyond them. Finally, those who commit errors, thinking that they will be able to rectify them afterward, will find that they cannot really repent. The habit of hypocrisy in which they have indulged will vitiate any future efforts to rectify their errors.

To be effective, repentance must be more than sorrow or remorse; it must include a determination never again to commit the transgression, and a rearrangement of one's way of life so as to avoid the temptation to fall into the transgression. Thus if a person has been guilty of theft, repentance requires not merely restitution of the stolen article, and a determination never to steal again, but also a study of the motives which led to the theft, and an endeavor to prevent them from being effective in the future.

One of the most important stimulants to the good life is the companionship of well-chosen friends. It is a duty to select friends with a view to their probable influence on character. The person who deliberately chooses wicked, companions, has only himself to blame if he finds himself falling into their manner of speech, and their daily habits.

The greatest possible deterrent from evil deeds or evil thoughts is the study of the Torah. By opening to man avenues of joy, creative endeavor, and happiness in the spiritual sphere, it removes from him the temptation to seek satisfaction of his human impulses to infringe on the rights of others or the commandments of God. If therefore a person finds himself facing temptation, he should turn more vigorously than ever to the study of the Torah.

Man differs from all other creatures, in that he is made "in the image of God." Because Judaism denies that God has any physical form, the image of God in this passage refers to man's mind. Created in the image of God, all persons must be accorded the respect due to this dignity which the Divine grace has accorded them. There can, therefore, be no differentiation between various human personalities in their status before God. From the time when the Prophet Amos declared, "Are ye not as the children of Ethiopians unto Me, O children of Israel" (9.7), until this day, Jewish religious teachers have continuously emphasized this doctrine. To Ben Azzai, the great teacher of the second century, the most inclusive principle of the whole Law is to be found in the verse, "In the day that God created man, in the likeness of God made He him, male and female created He them" (Genesis 5.1-2). He considered this verse uniquely important because it expresses unequivocally the equality and dignity of all human beings, irrespective of nationality, sex, color, creed, or genealogical origin.

Bearing in himself the image of God, man is also, according to Jewish doctrine, endowed with immortality. As conceived by most Jewish theologians, immortality implies the endless persistence of the human personality. This personality is believed to find its complete expression in ultimate reunion with God, and to lose all concern with the divisions, rivalries and antagonisms, characteristic of physical life.

The attainment of this endless communion with God is the highest reward which man can attain, and its loss is the greatest punishment he can suffer. The evil of wickedness consists, therefore, not merely in the harm which it does to a man in his mundane life, but in the fact that it deprives him of immortal existence. There are many rabbinic authorities who believe, as do members of other faiths, that certain sinful people may obtain immortal life, after having undergone temporary suffering after death. It is held in the Talmud that "the punishment of the wicked in Gehenna does not exceed twelve months." According to Maimonides, this punishment consists of the keen awareness by the soul of its failure to utilize its opportunities for the service of God, and is analogous to the shame sometimes felt by adults for unwise and unkind acts in their youth. But it is a fundamental principle in Judaism, formulated as an ethical norm by Antigonus of Socho, one of the founders of rabbinic Judaism, that men "should not be as servants, who serve their Master with the expectation of receiving reward, but rather as servants who serve their Master, without expectation of receiving reward." In other words, the belief in immortal life is accepted as a metaphysical and theological truth. However, it should not be considered a motive for proper conduct. Proper conduct should be based (as indicated hereafter) simply on love of God and the desire to see His will performed in the world.

The revelation of the Divine will, through the Law, the Prophets, and the Holy Writings, was a singular phenomenon in history. The people to whom this revelation was made was the people of Israel, of which only a remnant now survives, known as the Jewish people. The fact that the people of Israel received the Law and heard the Prophets does not, according to Jewish teaching, endow them with any special privileges. But it does place upon them special responsibilities. These responsibilities, to observe the Law, to study it, and to explain it, are expressed in the term, "The Chosen People." God did not choose Israel to be the recipient of any mundane goods or prerogatives. He chose Israel to be His suffering servant, to bear persecution with patience, and by precept and example, to bring His word to all peoples of the world.

As indicated in this discussion, there is a wide variety of interpretation among rabbinical scholars, both ancient and modern, with regard to the concepts of Judaism. In some instances, the differences of interpretation are so great that it is difficult to speak of the concept as being basically or universally Jewish or rabbinic. There are thus a number of concepts, each having its own limited authority and following.

This applies also to a degree to the fundamental beliefs which have been brought together in the best known Jewish creed, that of Maimonides. According to this creed, there are thirteen basic dogmas in Judaism. They are as follows:

1. The belief in God's existence.
2. The belief in His unity.
3. The belief in His incorporeality.
4. The belief in His timelessness.
5. The belief that He is approachable through prayer.
6. The belief in prophecy.
7. The belief in the superiority of Moses to all other prophets.
8. The belief in the revelation of the Law, and that the Law as contained in our Pentateuch is that revealed to Moses.
9. The belief in the immutability of the Law.
10. The belief in Divine providence.
11. The belief in Divine justice.
12. The belief in the coming of the Messiah.
13. The belief in the resurrection and human immortality.

This creed has been incorporated in the Jewish liturgy, in the famous hymn, *Yigdal.* Nevertheless, various distinguished authorities, including such teachers as Hasdai Crescas and Joseph Albo, rejected the classification of the doctrines, and even denied the basic character of some of the doctrines themselves. Because of this divergence of opinion among the most eminent authorities on the subject, traditional Judaism cannot be described as having a universally accepted creed or formulation of its dogmas.

This has led to the assertion that "Judaism has no dogmas." The assertion is true, only to the extent already indicated. On the other hand, as Rabbi Albo pointed out, the requirement that Jews observe the discipline of the Law implies the belief in God, in Revelation, and in Divine providence.

Orthodox and conservative Jews have in general followed the example of the ancient and mediaeval teachers in avoiding any effort to formulate a generally adopted Jewish creed, beyond the informal consensus of opinion found in traditional writings. As a result, there is still wide latitude of interpretation of Judaism both among orthodox and conservative Jews.

Reform Jews have tried to formulate a definite platform outlining the principles on which they agree, and which they believe basic to Judaism. The most recent platform is that adopted at a meeting of the Central Conference of American Rabbis (the organization of American reform rabbis) in 1937. In this platform no effort is made to indicate the way reform Judaism deviates from the orthodox or conservative interpretation of Judaism. And, indeed, the platform does not contain much to which orthodox and conservative groups can take exception. It is rather in its implications than by its direct statements, that it deviates from tradition.

Known as the Columbus Platform from the city in which the meeting was held, the statement reads as follows:

"In view of the changes that have taken place in the modern world and the consequent need of stating anew the teachings of Reform Judaism, the Central Conference of American Rabbis makes the following declaration of principles. It presents them not as a fixed creed but as a guide for the progressive elements of Jewry.

JUDAISM

I. Judaism and Its Foundations.

1. NATURE OF JUDAISM. Judaism is the historical religious experience of the Jewish people. Though growing out of Jewish life, its message is universal, aiming at the union and perfection of mankind under the sovereignty of God. Reform Judaism recognizes the principle of progressive development in religion and consciously applies this principle to spiritual as well as to cultural and social life.

Judaism welcomes all truth, whether written in the pages of Scripture or deciphered from the records of nature. The new discoveries of science, while replacing the older scientific views underlying our sacred literature, do not conflict with the essential spirit of religion as manifested in the consecration of man's will, heart and mind to the service of God and of humanity.

2. GOD. The heart of Judaism and its chief contribution to religion is the doctrine of the One, living God, Who rules the world through law and love. In Him all existence has its creative source and mankind its ideal of conduct. Though transcending time and space, He is the in-dwelling Presence of the world. We worship Him as the Lord of the universe and as our merciful Father.

3. MAN. Judaism affirms that man is created in the Divine image. His spirit is immortal. He is an active co-worker with God. As a child of God, he is endowed with moral freedom and is charged with the responsibility of overcoming evil and striving after ideal ends.

4. TORAH. God reveals Himself not only in the majesty, beauty and orderliness of nature, but also in the vision and moral striving of the human spirit. Revelation is a continuous process, confined to no one group and to no one age. Yet the people of Israel, through its prophets and sages, achieved unique insight in the realm of religious truth. The Torah, both written and oral, enshrines Israel's ever-growing consciousness of God and of the moral law. It preserves the historical precedents, sanctions and norms of Jewish life, and seeks to mould it in the

patterns of goodness and of holiness. Being products of historical processes, certain of its laws have lost their binding force with the passing of the conditions that called them forth. But as a depository of permanent spiritual ideals, the Torah remains the dynamic source of the life of Israel. Each age has the obligation to adapt the teachings of the Torah to its basic needs in consonance with the genius of Judaism.

5. ISRAEL. Judaism is the soul of which Israel is the body. Living in all parts of the world, Israel has been held together by the ties of common history, and above all, by the heritage of faith. Though we recognize in the group loyalty of Jews who have become estranged from our religious tradition, a bond which still unites them with us, we maintain that it is by its religion and for its religion that the Jewish people has lived. The non-Jew who accepts our faith is welcomed as a full member of the Jewish community.

In all lands where our people live, they assume and seek to share loyally the full duties and responsibilities of citizenship and to create seats of Jewish knowledge and religion. In the rehabilitation of Palestine, the land hallowed by memories and hopes, we behold the promise of renewed life for many of our brethren. We affirm the obligation of all Jewry to aid in its upbuilding as a Jewish homeland by endeavoring to make it not only a haven of refuge for the oppressed but also a center of Jewish culture and spiritual life.

Throughout the ages it has been Israel's mission to witness to the Divine in the face of every form of paganism and materialism. We regard it as our historic task to cooperate with all men in the establishment of the kingdom of God, of universal brotherhood, justice, truth and peace on earth. This is our Messianic goal.

II. Ethics.

6. ETHICS AND RELIGION. In Judaism religion and morality blend into an indissoluble unity. Seeking God means to strive after holiness, righteousness and goodness. The love of God is incomplete without the love of one's fellowmen. Judaism emphasizes the kinship of the human race, the sanctity and worth of human life and personality and the right of the individual to freedom and to the pursuit of his chosen vocation. Justice to all, irrespective of race. sect or class is the inalienable right and the inescapable obligation of all. The state and organized government exist in order to further these ends.

7. SOCIAL JUSTICE. Judaism seeks the attainment of a just society by the application of its teachings to the economic order, to industry and commerce, and to national and international affairs. It aims at the elimination of man-made misery and suffering, of poverty and degradation, of tyranny and slavery, of social inequality and prejudice, of ill-will and strife. It advocates the promotion of harmonious relations between warring classes on the basis of equity and justice, and the creation of conditions under which human personality may flourish. It pleads for the safeguarding of childhood against exploitation. It champions the cause of all who work and of their right to an adequate standard of living, as prior to the rights of property. Judaism emphasizes the duty of charity, and strives for a social order which will protect men against the material disabilities of old age, sickness and unemployment.

8. PEACE. Judaism, from the days of the prophets, has proclaimed to mankind the ideal of universal peace. The spiritual and physical disarmament of all nations has been one of its essential teachings. It abhors all violence and relies upon moral education, love and sympathy to secure human progress. It regards justice as the foundation of the well-being of nations and the condition of enduring peace. It urges organized international action for disarmament, collective security and world peace.

THE BASIC CONCEPTS OF JUDAISM

III. Religious Practice.

9. THE RELIGIOUS LIFE. Jewish life is marked by consecration to these ideals of Judaism. It calls for faithful participation in the life of the Jewish community as it finds expression in home, synagogue and school and in all other agencies that enrich Jewish life and promote its welfare.

The Home has been and must continue to be a stronghold of Jewish life, hallowed by the spirit of love and reverence, by moral discipline and religious observance and worship.

The Synagogue is the oldest and most democratic institution in Jewish life. It is the prime communal agency by which Judaism is fostered and preserved. It links the Jews of each community and unites them with all Israel.

The perpetuation of Judaism as a living force depends upon religious knowledge and upon the Education of each new generation in our rich cultural and spiritual heritage.

Prayer is the voice of religion, the language of faith and aspiration. It directs man's heart and mind Godward, voices the needs and hopes of the community, and reaches out after goals which invest life with supreme value. To deepen the spiritual life of our people, we must cultivate the traditional habit of communion with God through prayer in both home and synagogue.

Judaism as a way of life requires in addition to its moral and spiritual demands, the preservation of the Sabbath, festivals and Holy Days, the retention and development of such customs, symbols and ceremonies as possess inspirational value, the cultivation of distinctive forms of religious art and music and the use of Hebrew, together with the vernacular, in our worship and instruction.

These timeless aims and ideals of our faith we present anew to a confused and troubled world. We call upon our fellow Jews to rededicate themselves to them, and, in harmony with all men, hopefully and courageously to continue Israel's eternal quest after God and His kingdom."

31

None of the basic doctrines of Judaism deals expressly with the teachings, principles, or leading personalities of the younger religions derived from it. As Judaism antedates the origin of both Christianity and Mohammedanism, its views regarding both faiths are simply negative: it has not accepted their teachings. This attitude does not, however, prevent Judaism from endeavoring to appraise the significance and value of other faiths as spiritual and moral phenomena. Rabbi Jacob Emden (1697-1776), one of the foremost teachers in the history of Judaism, summarized the general Jewish view regarding Christianity in the following words:

"It is, therefore, a customary observation with me that the man of Nazareth wrought a double kindness to the world: On the one hand he fully supported the Torah of Moses, as already shown, for not one of our sages spoke more fervently about the eternal duty to fulfil the Law. On the other hand he brought much good to the Gentiles (if only they do not overturn his noble intention for them, as certain stupid people, who did not grasp the ultimate purpose of the New Testament have done; in fact, just recently I saw a book from the press whose author did not know himself what he had written; because, had he known what he had written, then his silence would have been more becoming than his speaking, and he would not have wasted his money nor spoiled the paper and the ink uselessly; just as among us are to be found stupid scholars who know not between their right hand and their left in the written, nor in the oral law, but deceive the world with a tongue that speaks arrogantly; but there are highly educated men of intelligence among the Christians, even as there are among the students of our Torah a few outstanding individuals, men of lofty erudition). For he (the man of Nazareth) forbade idol-worship and removed the image-deities, and he held the people responsible for the seven commandments, lest they be like the animals of the field; he sought to perfect them with ethical qualities that are much more rigorous even than those of the Law of Moses (as is well known), a policy that was surely just for its own sake, since that is the most direct way to acquire good traits, . . .[4]

None of the articles of faith in the creed of Maimonides deals with the holiness of Jerusalem, as the Holy City, or Palestine; yet the concept that Jerusalem, as the Holy City, and Palestine, as the Holy Land, have a special relation to Israel and its religion is fundamental to all Judaism. Every prayer contains a petition for the welfare of the Holy City and the Holy Land, and it is a basic principle in Judaism that to provide for the settlement of Palestine is to fulfil one of the Biblical commandments. A Jew seeing a Palestinian city in ruins must recite the benediction of bereavement, for every member of the Jewish faith is expected to regard the desolation of the Holy Land as a personal loss.

In the course of the centuries since the destruction of the Jewish community of Palestine, many efforts have been made to resettle considerable numbers of Jews there, to reclaim its arable land, and to restore some of its ancient forests. Within recent decades, the increased persecution of the Jews in certain countries has made the resettlement of Palestine a matter of practical importance, as well as religious significance. The difficulty encountered in observing certain aspects of Judaism in other countries has also stimulated many to return to Palestine. As a result, there has developed in the Holy Land a community of about 600,000 Jews at the present time (1945).

[4] From Jacob Emden's Letter in his edition of *Seder Olam Rabba we-Sutta u-Megillath Taanith*, Hamburg, 1757. A translation of the whole text is given by Oscar Z. Fasman in "An Epistle on Tolerance by a 'Rabbinic Zealot'", in *Judaism in a Changing World*, ed. Rabbi Leo Jung, New York, 1939, pp. 121-136.

In this restored Palestinian community, Hebrew has once more become a spoken language. Hebrew literature flourishes; there has been a rapid development of Hebrew poetry and prose, a greatly stimulated interest in the study of the Holy Scriptures, the Talmud, and later Jewish literature. A considerable portion of the new settlers has devoted itself to agricultural pursuits and lives in "colonies." Many of these are situated in lands which have been reclaimed from the pestilential marshes which covered them since the Arabic conquest, and perhaps for generations before.

In 1917, the British government issued its famous Balfour Declaration, stating that, "His Majesty's Government view with favor the establishment in Palestine of a national home for the Jewish people." This Declaration was subsequently incorporated into the mandate for Palestine, given by the League of Nations to Great Britain. Under the terms of this mandate, the Jewish community in Palestine has enjoyed a certain degree of autonomy, enabling it to regulate in part its own educational system, as well as to administer certain aspects of Talmudic civil law. One of the results of the development of the new settlement in Palestine has been the creation of the Hebrew University in Jerusalem in which the language of instruction is Hebrew.

The sporadic efforts at a renascence of Hebrew as a living tongue, which had been made in different parts of the world during the past century, have received a great impetus from the developments in the Holy Land. At the present time, Hebrew is taught as a spoken language in a considerable number of Jewish communities in all parts of the world.

The group among the Jews who have been most active

in the development of Palestinian life are called Zionists. Among the Zionists, those who are especially interested in reestablishing Palestine as a center of Jewish religious life are called the *Mizrachi* (of the east). Many Jews who are not Zionists also regard the development in Palestine with much sympathy and hope. These are Jews who are convinced that the development of a flourishing Jewish community in Palestine might become an important contribution to the development of human life. These men point, for example, to the interesting manner in which men and women trained in European university life have returned to the simple life of agricultural settlements, finding full satisfaction in the sense of creation which this return has given them. Some of the experiments in communal life now being conducted in Palestine may have significance for other parts of the world.

The complexity of modern life has persuaded a considerable number of Zionists that the future of the Palestinian community and its full usefulness to the development of civilization, will be impeded unless that community has a far greater degree of self-government than it now enjoys. The political status of the Palestinian Jewish community has thus become a matter of discussion, both among Jews and between Jewish groups and the mandatory government. At the present time (October 1945), it is impossible to forecast the result of these discussions.

35

V. THE SYSTEM OF BLESSINGS

The fundamental concept of the Jewish ceremonial system is that God continually reveals Himself in nature, in history, and in man's daily life. Each ceremony seeks to emphasize some aspect of this Divine revelation, and thus becomes a special means for communion between man and God. By stressing the common dependence of all men on God, ceremonies strengthen the sense of human kinship. By drawing attention to the phenomena of Nature, they help develop man's sense of the esthetic, and increase his joy in the contemplation of beauty. By opening up vistas of achievement and satisfaction, they help free him from subjection to material needs and desires, and enable him to fulfil his higher potentialities.

Jewish tradition has evolved the system of ritual blessings as an effective means for achieving continual realization of God's manifestation in the world. According to rabbinic Law, a Jew is expected to recite a blessing whenever he enjoys any particular aspect of the world. When he awakes, he thanks God for having created the day, for having granted him the power of sight, for the creation of the earth, for the gift of clothes, for the power to walk, and for the renewal of his strength in sleep. He also thanks God that he is not an idolator nor a slave. Mindful of the severity of woman's lot in the world, and her consequent inability to fulfil many of the commandments, the man recites a benediction that he is male, rather than female;

while a woman thanks God that He "has created her according to His will." The observant Jew also recites some verses from Scripture and a passage from the Talmud. Before doing so, he thanks God for the revelation through the Law, and for the commandment to study the Law.

Before sitting down to his morning meal, he is expected to recite the prayers described below. At the meal itself, both before and after eating, he recites prescribed blessings. These blessings are repeated at every meal. The blessing at the beginning of the meal is the simple benediction, "Blessed art Thou, O Lord, our God, King of the Universe, Who dost bring bread out of the ground." The blessing after the meal consists of four paragraphs. The first is devoted to thanks to God for supplying all men and indeed all living things with their daily needs. The second is an expression of gratitude for His having caused ancient Israel to inherit the Holy Land. The third is a prayer for the restoration of Jerusalem. The fourth paragraph is a blessing of God for His continued goodness to all men.

When three people eat together, the blessing after the meal is recited in unison. Such a group is popularly called *mezuman* (prepared), because before he begins, the person reciting the grace asks whether all are prepared for it. If there is a guest at the table, the recital of the grace is assigned to him. If there are several guests, the most learned is expected to recite it. At the end of the grace, the person reciting it invokes a blessing on his host and hostess: "May the All-merciful bless the master and mistress of this house, them, and their house, and their children, and all that is theirs; us, and all that is ours, as our ancestors, Abraham, Isaac, and Jacob were blessed."

At every meal which is attended by three or more peo-

ple, "words of the Torah" should be spoken. If this is
done, the meal becomes sanctified, and "it is as though
they have partaken of the table of the Lord," i.e., of a
sacrificial meal. In order to fulfil this requirement, it is
customary to recite a psalm at every meal. Psalm 137 is
recited on weekdays, and Psalm 126 on Sabbaths, festivals,
and half-holidays. On festival occasions, and other occasions when it is possible, the recital of these psalms is
supplemented by discussions of questions related to religious or spiritual life. To emphasize the sacred character
of the meal, it is considered proper to wash one's hands
both before and after it, just as was done at sacrificial
meals in the Temple.

In addition to these blessings which are recited virtually
every day, there are special blessings to be repeated, such
as those for the sight of the trees in the spring, a view of
the ocean, a meeting with a friend after a long absence,
the appearance of meteors, lightning, the rainbow, the new
moon, the sight of strange creatures, the acquisition of new
clothes,[5] the acquisition of new possessions, and the recep-
tion of good news. On hearing bad news, a special benediction must be recited, accepting the Divine judgment.
This benediction, "Blessed art Thou, O Lord our God,
King of the Universe, the true Judge," is also recited on
the occasion of any bereavement. Finally, there are prayers
prescribed for the afternoon and the evening (see below)
and a concluding prayer at bedtime.

[5] This blessing is not recited when wearing leather garments because
it is not considered fitting to thank God for life when using material
produced at the cost of life.

VI. THE SYNAGOGUE AND THE PRAYERS

In ancient times, the center of Jewish worship was at the Temple in Jerusalem, where sacrifices were offered in accordance with the prescriptions of the Law. But there were prophets in Israel even in the days of priests, and the prophets frequently organized prayer-meetings at which people assembled for devotion and religious exhortation. From these meetings eventually the synagogue was to develop; and subsequently the church and the mosque. As the 'chief element in the Temple service was sacrifice, so that of the synagogue was prayer. The precedent for prayer was, of course, an ancient one. Abraham interceded with God on behalf of the people of Sodom. Fearing attack, Jacob uttered the beautiful prayer which contains the memorable words, "I am not worthy of all the mercies, and of all the truth, which Thou hast shown Thy servant; for with my staff I passed this Jordan, and now I am become two camps" (Genesis 32.11). Hannah came to the Temple to petition and praise the Lord. Indeed, Solomon in his dedication service referred to the Temple essentially as a house of prayer in which men would supplicate the Lord.

Even before the Exile, gatherings for prayer were to be found among the people. The Babylonian exile and the return to Palestine, however, were especially instrumental in strengthening the synagogue. The institution offered not only an opportunity for pious devotion but for study as well, for it was at these assemblies that Scripture was read and explained. The assembly for worship which proved of such importance in Palestine while the Temple at Jerusalem still endured, became indispensable when the Temple was destroyed. Since that time, the synagogue has been the sole sanctuary of the Jewish people.

The architecture of the synagogue varies according to country and age. The essential elements of the institution are the Ark containing the scroll of the Law, a stand for the reader of the service who faces the Ark, and in most traditional synagogues a second stand in the middle of the gathering for the reading of the Law. In a large number of American synagogues, no provision is made for this second stand.

In accordance with the tradition derived from the Temple in Jerusalem, the "court of women" is separated from that of the men in traditional synagogues. It is either marked off by a partition, or is situated in a gallery. Again, a considerable number of American synagogues, including most of the conservative synagogues and all the reform synagogues, have deviated from tradition in this respect, and permit men and women to sit together.

No human figures may be used in the decoration of the synagogue. However, it is permitted, and has even become customary, to depict on the Ark and elsewhere in the building a lion or an eagle, suggesting the latter half of the rabbinical injunction, "Be bold as the leopard, fleet as the deer, light as the eagle, and strong as the lion, to do the will of thy Father who is in Heaven." In many synagogues, the passage is inscribed over the reader's stand. It is also usual to place over the Ark a symbolic representation of the two tablets containing the Ten Commandments. Generally, only the first words of each of the

Commandments is inscribed on the tablets. The so-called Shield (or Star) of David which is found in many synagogue buildings, and otherwise in Jewish symbolism, is of unknown origin. But its use can be traced back to rabbinic times. -

In many synagogues, there is to be found over the reader's desk a candelabrum, or two candelabra, symbolic of that which stood in the Temple of Jerusalem. But because it is forbidden to set up in a synagogue an exact replica of the utensils used in the ancient Temple, such candelabra usually have instead of seven, eight or nine, sometimes fourteen branches.

In further deference to the unique sanctity of the Temple, kneeling or prostrating oneself in the synagogue worship is forbidden, except on special occasions in the services of the New Year's Day and the Day of Atonement. Prayers are said either standing or sitting. It is customary to bow one's head on entering the synagogue, and while reciting certain portions of the prayers. In orthodox and conservative synagogues, men pray with covered heads. It is considered a violation of custom to perform any act of worship, including study of the Scripture or the Talmud, with uncovered head. This custom derives from that prescribed for the priests of the Temple in Exodus 28.40-42. The custom has been abandoned in most American reform synagogues.

It has become customary to speak of reform synagogues and conservative synagogues, as Temples. This change of name does not imply any difference other than those already indicated.

The essential element in the synagogue is, of course, not the building, but the community. Public worship may be conducted in a building, or out of doors. But it can be held only in the presence of a congregation, which theoretically consists of a minimum of ten heads of households. For the purpose of prayer, and because of the difficulty in finding ten heads of households in very small communities, ten males (over thirteen years of age) are considered heads of households. The assembly of ten such people is called a *minyan* (quorum) sufficient for public service.

Any adult male Jew may lead the congregation in public prayers. The rabbi participates simply as a member of the congregation. It has become usual in large congregations to appoint a special official to read the prayers, especially those of the Sabbaths and festivals. Such a reader is called a *hazzan*. In some congregations the *hazzan* has a choir to assist him. In orthodox congregations, this choir consists only of men; in some conservative and in all reform congregations, women are also admitted to the choir. A number of passages in the service are traditionally sung by the whole congregation in unison. The tendency of modern orthodox and conservative synagogues is to extend this practice to include a much larger part of the service.

In addition to the *hazzan,* the congregation may require the services of a special reader for the Scriptures. He must be able not only to read the consonantal text of the scroll without the aid of vowels, but must be expert in the traditional system of cantillation of the Scriptures. This system of chanting is of great historical interest, because at least certain parts of it, particularly that prescribed for use on the High Holy Days, are obviously of great antiquity.

The duty of looking after the arrangements for the service, that is, seeing that the scrolls are prepared for reading, that the prayer-books are available for the worshippers, and that the members having special duties during the service know their assignments, devolves generally on a functionary called the *shammash* (sexton).

In addition to these officials who generally are remunerated for their duties, American congregations usually have lay officers, a president, one or more vice-presidents, a secretary, a treasurer, and board of directors, upon whom devolves the responsibility for the material well-being of the congregation.

As already indicated, tradition expects every member of the Jewish faith to pray at least three times a day: in the morning, *shaharit;* in the afternoon, *minhah;* and in the evening, *ma'arib.* On Sabbaths and festivals, an additional prayer is assigned for morning service, called *musaf* (addition), to commemorate the special sacrifices which were offered on such days at the Temple in Jerusalem. On the Day of Atonement, a fifth prayer is recited at sunset. This prayer, in some respects the most solemn of the year, is called *ne'ilah* (closing), and commemorates the service held at the Temple when its gates were closed at the end of the sacred day.

All of these prayers should, so far as possible, be recited at a public service. But if it is difficult to arrange to participate in a public service, they can be recited in private (with omissions of certain portions which belong only to the public service). Most observant Jews attend synagogue services at least on the Sabbaths and holidays; every orthodox and conservative synagogue endeavors to arrange for public services also on weekdays.

The essential element in all these services is the prayer called *'amidah* (literally, standing, so called because one must rise to recite it). The weekday version of this prayer consists of nineteen paragraphs. But in the original Palestinian form, given it by Rabban Gamaliel II eighteen centuries ago, it contained only eighteen paragraphs; and the prayer is therefore frequently called *shemoneh 'esreh* (eighteen).

At all services, except the evening service, this prayer is recited twice. It is first recited in an undertone by each individual in the congregation; and then aloud by the reader, on behalf of the congregation. The first and last three paragraphs of the *'amidah* are identical for all the services. The first paragraphs consist of confessions of faith in God as the God of the Patriarchs, Abraham, Isaac, and Jacob; as the One Who gives strength to the living and new life to the dead; and as the Holy One, Who has no equal. The final paragraphs include a prayer for the return of God's presence to Jerusalem; an expression of gratitude for all the goodness God has shown us; and a prayer for peace.

On the festivals, it is the rule in all orthodox and in many conservative synagogues, that the descendants of the ancient Aaronid priests bless the people before the final paragraphs of the public reading of the *musaf 'amidah*. The formula used in this blessing is that prescribed in Numbers 6.22-27, "May the Lord bless thee and keep thee; may the Lord cause His countenance to shine upon thee and be gracious unto thee; may the Lord lift His countenance upon thee and give thee peace."

Before reciting this blessing, the descendants of Aaron who are in the synagogue, remove their shoes (as was the custom in the Temple in Jerusalem). The Levites who are present in the synagogue then wash the hands of the Aaronids, who thereupon step forward, face the congregation, and recite the ancient blessing.

The middle paragraphs of the daily *'amidah* contain

petitions for the fulfilment of various needs for the grant-ing of wisdom, repentance, and forgiveness, for the re-demption of Israel, for the healing of the sick, for pros-perous years, for the gathering of the dispersed, for the restoration of the Sanhedrin, for the suppression of tyranny, for the protection of the righteous, for the re-building of Jerusalem, for the coming of the Messiah, and for the acceptance of prayer.

All of the prayers are for the good of the whole com-munity. Petitions for private needs may be inserted in their appropriate place. For example, the prayer for a sick person may be included in the general prayer for the sick of the world.

On Sabbaths and festivals, these petitions for the satis-faction of material wants are necessarily omitted; for it is forbidden to consider material needs on such days. On these occasions there is a single prayer for a complete rest on the Sabbath, and for happiness on the festival.

At every service the silent reading of the *'amidah* ends with the prayer which begins: "O, my God! Guard my tongue from evil, and my lips from speaking guile. To such as curse me, let me be dumb. Let me, indeed, be as dust unto all. . . . If any design evil against me, speedily make their counsel of no effect, and frustrate their in-tentions."

At the morning and evening services the *'amidah* is pre-ceded by the recital of the *Shema* and the various bene-dictions with it. The *Shema* begins with the verse, "Hear, O Israel, the Lord is our God, the Lord is One" (Deuter-onomy 6.4), and includes Deuteronomy 6.5-9, 11.13-21, and Numbers 15.37-41. In all services the recital of the *Shema* is preceded by a blessing of God for His revelation in the Law, and is followed by a blessing for His redemption of Israel from Egypt. In the morning, there is also a blessing for the light, in the evening a blessing for the darkness.

Each of the services begins and ends with the recital of the *Kaddish,* an Aramaic prayer for the coming of the Kingdom of God. It is, in effect, a prayer on behalf of the congregation by the reader before he enters on his service and after he ends it. Its essential element is its first section, reading: "May the great Name of God be exalted and sanctified in the world which He created according to His will, and may He cause His Kingdom to come, in your lives and in your days, and in the lives of all the House of Israel; speedily, and in a short time. Amen."

In the course of time, it has become customary to recite this prayer also at other parts of the service. Since the Middle Ages, it has been usual also to recite it during the year of a bereavement, and on the anniversary of the death of one's parents.

In the morning services held on Mondays and Thursdays (the market days of ancient Palestine, when a larger congregation would be available than on other weekdays), as well as on Sabbaths, festivals, new moons, and fast days, portions of the Five Books of Moses are read from the sacred scrolls. The readings are so arranged that the whole of the Pentateuch is covered within a year. On Sabbath and festival mornings, as well as at the afternoon services on fast days, selections from the Books of the Prophets are read in addition to those from the Torah. Such a portion is called the *haftarah,* and the person reading it is called the *maftir.*

As stated above, the reading from the Torah is now assigned to a special functionary. In ancient times, the members of the congregation would each ascend in turn to perform this duty. In deference to this tradition, it is still customary to call various individuals to read special portions of the Torah, though they merely repeat the words *sotto voce,* while the reading aloud is the duty of the professional reader. There are seven such participants in the Sabbath morning reading of the Torah; six in that of the Day of Atonement, five in those of the festivals; four in those of new moons and the festival weeks; and three at all other services when the Torah is read. Whenever the Torah is read, the first person to be called must be a descendant of Aaron, if there is any in the synagogue. The second to be called must be a Levite, and the others are chosen from the remainder of the congregation. When the prophetic portions are read at morning services of the Sabbaths and festivals, an additional person is called. He may be either an Aaronid, a Levite, or any other Israelite.

There are certain occasions when it is considered an especial obligation to participate in the public reading of the Torah. The most important of these are the Sabbath succeeding one's thirteenth birthday (see below); the Sabbath preceding one's marriage; the anniversaries of the death of one's parents; and the Sabbath following one's recovery from illness or escape from danger. It is usual for persons who are thus required to participate in the reading of the Scriptures, to be assigned to the *haftarah*. A person who reads the Torah after recovering from illness or escape from danger, recites a special blessing on the occasion, saying: "Blessed be Thou, O Lord, our God, King of the Universe, Who dost grant kindness to the undeserving, and Who hast granted me every good." The congregation, hearing the blessing, responds, "He Who has granted thee kindness, may He ever continue to grant thee kindness."

47

The language of the prayers of the traditional service is for the most part Hebrew. However, a number of prayers are in Aramaic which was the vernacular of the Jews in the first centuries of the Christian era in Palestine and Babylonia. At the present time the proportion of Hebrew to some other language (in America, for example, English) will vary with the individual congregation. But everywhere some portions of the public service are read in Hebrew.

According to rabbinic tradition, it is customary for men to wear a prayer-shawl called the *tallit* (garment) during the morning prayers. This prayer-shawl is a square or oblong woolen cloth, with fringe at each of its four corners. It is a very ancient garment, probably worn in antiquity as a cloak. The purpose of the fringe (*ṣiṣit*) at the four corners is explained in the Bible: "That ye may look upon it and remember all the commandments of the Lord and do them . . . and be holy unto the Lord your God" (Numbers 15.39-40). In addition, it is customary for men to don the *tephillin* (phylacteries) during the morning services on weekdays. These *tephillin* consist of two boxes of parchment to which are attached long leather straps. In the boxes are deposited little strips of parchment with the contents of Exodus 11.16, 13.1-10; Deuteronomy 6.4-9, 11.13-21. The Bible also gives the meaning of this symbol: "And it shall be for a sign unto thee upon thy hand, and for a memorial between thine eyes, that the Law of the Lord may be in thy mouth; for with a strong hand hath the Lord brought thee out of Egypt" (Exodus 13.9). To the ancient rabbis the *tephillin* on the head, and on the left arm close to the heart, represented the concentration of the intellect and the emotion on the Divine. As Maimonides subsequently expressed it: "As long as the *tephil-*

lin are on the head and on the arm of a man, he is modest and God-fearing; he will not be attracted by hilarity or idle talk, and will have no evil thoughts, but will devote all his thoughts to truth and righteousness."

Two of these Biblical sections, namely Deuteronomy 6.4-9 and 11.13-21, are also inscribed on pieces of parchment which are placed in receptacles, attached by the observant Jew to the doorposts of every room. Such receptacles are called *mezuzot* (literally, doorposts). These inscriptions are intended to remind man, as he enters home or leaves it, of the unity of God and of the duty of loving Him.

VII. THE SABBATH AND THE FESTIVALS

While according to the Jewish faith God's presence can be felt at any time and place, there are times, just as there are places, which through their associations have become especially propitious for communion with God. Of these the most important are the holy days and the fast days. .The holy days, according to the Jewish ritual, are the *Shabbat* or Sabbath, celebrated on the seventh day of each week, *Pesach* (Passover), *Shabuot* (Pentecost), *Rosh Ha-Shanah* (the Jewish religious New Year's Day), *Yom Kippur* (Day of Atonement), and *Sukkot* (Tabernacles).

In order that these days may be devoted as completely as possible to the spiritual life, work is forbidden on them. This prohibition includes not only all gainful occupation, but also household tasks.

As a result of these various prohibitions, the Sabbath and festivals become virtually periods of cessation of all labor on the part of observant Jews. Because of the difficulties involved in maintaining this rigid discipline in an industrial society like our own, many Jews otherwise very observant, do not refrain from all labor on the Sabbath. Nevertheless, even among these a large number set aside the free hours of the day for spiritual contemplation and for prayer, and mark the Sabbath with the ceremonials devoted to it.

Theoretically, observant Jews should not benefit from the willingness of members of other faiths to perform tasks

for them on the Sabbath day. But because of the severity
of the winters in Northern and Central Europe, and the
consequent danger of disease, it became customary in the
Middle Ages to permit people who were not Jews to kindle
the fire for the Jews on the Sabbath. As a result, in time
Christian and Moslem boys came to look after the heating
of Jewish homes on the Sabbath. In recent centuries,
people of other faiths also extinguish lights for Jews on
the Sabbath, on the theory that rest is as imperative for
health as warmth.

In the Jewish religious calendar, the observance of
festivals begins a little before sunset on the preceding day.
Because no fire is kindled on the Sabbath, it has been
customary from time immemorial for Jewish housewives
to conclude all their household arrangements for the day
of rest by preparing the lights, which have therefore become known as the "Sabbath lights." The great antiquity
of this usage, and the significance which came to be attached to it, have sanctified it, and consequently in modern
Jewish homes the Sabbath candles are lit, even though
other means of illumination are available and are in use.
Many a Jew has tender memories of the sight of his mother
lighting the Sabbath candles. As their light is not to be
enjoyed before the blessing, the Jewish mother with her
hands over her eyes recites, "Blessed are Thou, O Lord
our God, King of the Universe, Who has sanctified us with
Thy commandments, and commanded us to kindle the
Sabbath lights."

In the absence of the mother of the household, the lights
are kindled by someone acting for her. If by chance the
lights have not been kindled on a Sabbath, it is customary
for her to kindle an additional light before every Sabbath
afterward throughout her life.

The beauty and impressiveness of the custom of the Sabbath lights has caused it to be extended, so that similar lights are now kindled also on festivals for which the use of fire is permitted, and therefore there is no special reason for lighting candles before dark. In kindling the lights on the seasonal festivals, however, the mother recites the special prayer of thanks for life called *sheheheyanu* (Who has kept us alive), "Blessed art Thou, O Lord our God, King of the Universe, Who hast caused us to live, and attain this day."

Evening services are held in the synagogue on the eve of festivals and Sabbaths at dusk. After the services, the members of the family return home for the Sabbath meal. On the table are placed a flask of wine and two loaves of bread. The Sabbath loaf of bread is called by its Hebrew name, *hallah* (plural, *hallot,* or as popularly pronounced, *hallos*). The two loaves of bread are said to symbolize the double share of manna which God granted the Israelites in the wilderness on Fridays to provide for the Sabbath (Exodus 16.5). It is customary in many localities to prepare these loaves in an especially attractive form, made of twisted strands of dough. On festivals, the bread is further enriched by a plentiful supply of raisins. (On Passover, as will be seen below, the bread is replaced by unleavened cakes.) The loaves of bread are covered with a napkin, and the head of the household takes a cup of wine, and recites over it the blessing called the *kiddush,* or sanctification of the day. This blessing consists of a prayer of thanks to God for the gift of the wine, and then for the gift of the special festival. The head of the household drinks some of the wine, and distributes the rest among the others present. On seasonal festivals, the *kiddush* also includes the blessing *sheheheyanu,* mentioned above. Then follows the ritual washing of the hands, the blessing for the bread, the breaking of the bread, the meal itself, the special hymns of the Sabbath or the festival meal, and the blessing after the meal.

In many conservative and reform congregations, special services on Sabbath eve are held after the Sabbath meal. These services are intended to enable those men and women who because of modern industrial conditions do not attend the traditional service at dusk, to commune with God during the course of the holy day. The ritual used at these services varies considerably. In some congregations, it is the usual Sabbath eve service. In others, it consists of the hymns sung at the Sabbath evening meal. In virtually all congregations where such services are held, it is customary to include a sermon by the rabbi.

The Sabbath and festival morning service are longer than those of the weekdays, and occupy most of the morning hours. As it is considered improper to eat before prayers, traditional Jewish homes do not provide for any breakfast on Sabbaths or festivals. The ritual of the noon meal is very similar to that of the evening. It includes a blessing over the cup of wine, the blessing for the bread, the breaking and distribution of the bread, the meal itself, and the blessing after the meal.

It is customary in observant homes to arrange for another meal to be served in the late afternoon of the Sabbath day, so as to complete three Sabbath meals. This third meal is called *seudah shelishit* (third meal), or more popularly and less correctly, *shalosh seudot* (three meals). No wine need be drunk before the third meal, but the blessing for the bread is recited as usual.

In Palestine, it has become customary within the last decade, as a result of the influence of the famous Hebrew poet, Chayyim Nahman Bialik, to substitute for the third meal, a public gathering, preferably one at which refreshments are served, called *oneg shabbat*, the delight of the Sabbath. The practice of holding such gatherings has become an institution in other parts of the world, and is rapidly being adopted by congregations in this country. It is an effort to bring people together on the Sabbath afternoon for a discussion of religious, literary, or ethical problems, while participating in a symbolic Sabbath meal.

The Sabbath is concluded after sunset with a blessing called *habdalah* (division, that is, marking the division between the Sabbath and the weekdays). A flask of wine and a box of incense are set on the table, and a light is struck. It seems appropriate that the workaday week should begin with the taste of the wine, the odor of the incense, and the appearance of the light, which, satisfying three different senses, increase man's awareness of his dependence on God for all his needs. The blessing consists, therefore, of thanks to God for the gift of the wine, of the incense, and of the light; and ends with further thanks for the division between the Sabbath and the weekdays. It is customary to let the cup of wine for *habdalah* overflow, as a symbol that the happiness of the week may likewise overflow. It is also customary to use a candle with three or four wicks (resembling an ancient torch) for the light of the *habdalah*.

The same ritual of *habdalah* is recited in the synagogue, in order to provide for those who cannot observe it in their homes. It also concludes the Day of Atonement, and with the exception of the blessing for the light, all the other festivals.

The rigid prohibition of work on the Sabbath does not, as is frequently believed, make it a day of gloom for the observant Jew. On the contrary, the complete release from all mundane concern, the concentration on the study of the Torah, and the joy in the sense of communion with God, make it a day of great, though perhaps indescribable, delight. To participate in the observance of the Sabbath gives such happiness, that one of the prayers added to the blessing after the meal on the day, asks that Paradise may be one long Sabbath. As twilight descends on Sabbath afternoon, some feel an ineffable sense of yearning and lonesomeness, which the mystics among the Jews have characterized as the loss of part of one's soul.

Aside from the Sabbath, the major Jewish festivals are Passover, Pentecost, New Year's Day, the Day of Atonement, and the Feast of the Tabernacles. Each of these is according to tradition a day of judgment for all mankind. "On Passover the world is judged regarding its grain; on Pentecost regarding the fruits of the tree; on New Year's Day (and also on the Day of Atonement) all creatures pass before God as in a military review; and on Tabernacles they are judged concerning the rain."

While this consciousness of judgment gives an air of solemnity to all the festivals, the three festivals of the ancient pilgrimages, Passover, Pentecost, and Tabernacles, are primarily periods of joy. The manner in which the joy of the festival is combined with the sense of solemnity and judgment before God is difficult to explain to the uninitiate. The festival prayers, as well as the special melodies which in certain rituals accompany them, reflect a feeling of awe, arising from the sense of communion with God as Judge and Ruler of the universe; yet united with this feeling and permeating it, is a sense of confidence that His judgment will be one of mercy rather than severity, as that of a father upon his child. The joy of the festival is thus prevented from becoming one of physical pleasure or self-indulgence. Ideally conceived, it is a joy arising largely from participation in synagogue and home rituals, which bring about a closer communion with God.

The significance of each festival is enhanced through the natural and historical interpretations associated with it. All of them are intended to increase man's faith in God by reference to His revelation in the natural order, and also in the succession of human events. Their symbols are particularly significant in an industrial and commercial civilization, where man tends to be separated from nature; and their reflection of the Divine purpose in history gives one strength in times of international crisis, and fills one with humility in moments of peace and prosperity. The purpose of the festivals may thus be said to place human life in both its cosmic and historical perspectives. They enable Man to see himself both as part of Nature and as distinguished through the providence of God.

Passover, occurring on the full moon of the first month of spring (toward the end of March or the beginning of April), is the great festival of the re-birth of Nature, and also commemorates historically the exodus from Egypt. The concentration of Jews in the cities during past centuries has tended to minimize the agricultural aspect of the Passover. Nevertheless, certain ancient customs emphasizing the seasonal character of the festival are still observed. The first month of spring in Palestine marks the end of the rainy season and the beginning of the dry season. In this dry season, the crops are saved from destruction by a heavy dew each night. Hence Passover has become a festival of prayer for the dew, and the *musaf* (additional) prayer of the first day of Passover is dedicated to petition for copious dew on the earth. The second night

of Passover was celebrated in ancient Palestine as the
beginning of the barley harvest. In accordance with Leviticus 23.14, no part of the new crop might be eaten before
that night, when the first sheaf was harvested and prepared
as a sacrifice to God. While the observance of the sacrifice
is impossible today, it is still customary for men of great
piety in European communities to avoid eating the new
grain before the second night of Passover. All traditional
Jewish communities mark the second night of Passover as
the beginning of the barley harvest in ancient Palestine;
and following a literal interpretation of Leviticus 23.15-16,
include in the daily evening service, an enumeration of
the forty-nine days from that night until Pentecost, the
festival of the wheat harvest.

But the historical significance of Passover as commemorating the Exodus and the promulgation of the idea of
freedom in the world, has far overshadowed the agricultural phase of the festival. The ceremonies prescribed for
the festival in Scripture and the additional rules established by the rabbis, have as their purpose emphasis on the
idea of human liberty and equality. The most obvious
characteristic of the festival is the use of the unleavened
bread (called *maṣṣah*, pronounced *matzah*), the bread of
affliction (Deuteronomy 16.3), recalling to each Jew, the
bondage of his ancestry in Egypt, and emphasizing by
inference his equality with the humblest and most oppressed of men. The significance of the custom has become
such that it is observed with greater precision than almost
any other law in Scripture. Observant Jews abstain from
eating not only any leavened bread on the festival, but
even any food which might conceivably have a taste or
trace of leaven. The grain used for *maṣṣah* is carefully
examined to see whether any of it has become leaven. The

57

examination is usually performed by a rabbi, who takes a sampling of the grain. If he finds that none of those in his sample has become leaven, the contents of that granary may be used for Passover. After the examination, the grain must be carefully guarded against any moistening, which might cause it to leaven. The mills in which it is ground are carefully scoured and purified from all leaven. The flour is then again guarded against moisture, until it is brought to the bakery. In the bakery, expert mechanics and especially devised machines make it possible to prepare the dough and bake it with such speed that it is quite impossible for any leavening to take place. No salt, and of course no yeast or any material other than flour and water, enter into the making of the *maṣṣah*. After the *maṣṣah* has been baked, it may be ground again into flour, which can then be used for making pastries and other dishes for consumption on the Passover. Such flour is called *matzah meal*.

Traditional observance of the Passover requires that no prepared food such as dried fruits or vegetables shall be used, unless it has been made certain that not a speck of flour attaches to them. For this reason, raisins, prunes, coffee, pepper, and similar foods are used by observant Jews during the Passover only if they are prepared under the supervision of a rabbi. Dried peas or beans may not be eaten under any circumstances. Ashkenazic Jews do not eat rice on Passover, though following the tradition of their ancestors, Jews of Sephardic descent consider it permitted.

Special cooking utensils and dishes are set aside for the Passover week, so that no utensils or dishes which have contained leaven will come into contact with the Passover food. Families which cannot afford a complete set of special dishes may cleanse their metal utensils and certain types of glassware for use during the Passover week. Such cleansing must follow the ritual prescriptions, and should be done only after consultation with a rabbi.

To purify the home from all leaven before the Passover, it is customary on the night before the festival eve to "search the house" for any bread or leaven. In earlier ages, this searching had the practical purpose of discovering such leaven, for in the simple one-room homes of the ancient east it was possible to delay the removal of leaven until the night before the festival. In modern homes, this cleaning naturally occupies several days or even weeks, and the ritual searching for the leaven is virtually a formal custom. Nevertheless, the custom is observed in most orthodox and conservative homes. The head of the household searches for the leaven, removes all he finds, and puts it aside until the next morning, when it must be burned during the first quarter of the day, that is, around 9:00 a.m. After that hour it is forbidden to eat leavened food or to own it. As it is usually difficult to destroy all the leavened food in a home and quite impossible to dispose of all the dishes used for leavened food, it is customary among many groups of observant Jews to transfer the title of their leavened food to the rabbi of the community during the Passover week. The rabbi in turn technically transfers the title to this food to a member of another faith.

On the first and second nights of Passover, a unique home service is celebrated. This celebration is called the seder (order), because the whole meal follows a prescribed ritual order. There is a festive gathering of the whole family in each household, and strangers who are separated from their families are invited as guests. In communities where the number of strangers is considerable, provision is frequently made for a group *seder* at a public institution.

The poignant beauty of the *seder* service leaves an indelible impression on every Jewish child who participates in it. It is in effect a pageant in which ancient Palestinian life is recreated in as detailed and precise a form as possible. The head of the household (or at a public celebration, the leader of the service) is provided with a divan on which after the fashion of the ancients, he may recline during the meal and the celebration. According to some rituals, he is expected to don a *kittel,* a white linen garment worn in ancient Jerusalem on festive days.

The service followed at the *seder* is described in a special prayer-book, the *Passover Haggadah.* This book contains directions for arranging the Passover dish to be placed before the master of the house, and detailed instructions for the procedure during the service.

One of the most significant elements in the *seder* is its highly developed pedagogical technique. In order to impress the child, he is urged to observe the various ceremonies which are conducted, and to ask for an explanation of them. As the service is recited it thus becomes fundamentally a reply to these questions. The child is informed that the celebration is in memory of the Exodus from Egypt; he is told the story of the Israelite bondage; of the redemption of the people through the mercy of God; and is taught to respect the liberty which he has inherited through this redemption.

At the end of the Passover meal, which is eaten in the course of the *seder,* the door is opened as a symbol of the entry of Elijah the Prophet. A cup of wine, "the cup of Elijah," is filled, the whole company rise, and cry, "Blessed is he who has come!" The concept that Elijah, the immortal prophet, visits every Jewish home on the Passover eve, emphasizes the significance of the festival as a symbol of eternal freedom, as well as memorial of a past emancipation; for Elijah is the prophet who, according to the words of Malachi, will be the precursor of God's establishing His Kingdom on earth, at the end of days.

The *seder* ends with the recital of various psalms, the tasting of a fourth and final cup of wine, the singing of various hymns, and finally with popular songs, dating from mediaeval times. In many communities, the head of the household concludes the whole service by reading the Biblical Book, Canticles (The Song of Songs). The joyful spirit of youth, which permeates that book, seems appropriate for the spring festival; and the allegorical meaning imposed on it, as an epic of God's relation to Israel, are particularly fitting for recollection on the festival of the Exodus.

The period between Passover and Pentecost is now observed in many Jewish communities as one of partial mourning, because it is traditionally described as the time when the disciples of Rabbi Akiba, one of the foremost teachers of the Talmud, died. Except for certain special days within the period, no weddings are celebrated by observant Jews; and they also abstain from listening to music, attending theatres, or participating in other pleasures.

The thirty-third day of this period, called *Lag Ba'Omer* (literally, the thirty-third day of the *Omer*), is a half-holiday, devoted to the celebration of weddings and other festivities. It is sometimes said to be the anniversary of the death of Rabbi Simeon ben Yohai, the foremost of Rabbi Akiba's disciples, which is marked in this way as the occasion of his translation to the Heavenly Academy. To this day it is therefore customary in Palestine to mark the day with a festive pilgrimage to the supposed grave of Rabbi Simeon in Meron, a village of Galilee.

Pentecost or *Shabuot* (occurring toward the end of May or the beginning of June) is described in Scripture primarily as the festival of the wheat harvest (Exodus 23.16). But it also commemorates the Revelation on Mount Sinai, and is therefore the festival of the Ten Commandments. The reading of the Law assigned to it covers the chapter telling the story of the Revelation (Exodus 19.20); the liturgy of the day is also dedicated in part to commemorating this incident. In many orthodox congregations, the evening of the first night of Pentecost is spent in reading Scriptural passages. Among some especially pious Jews, it is customary to remain awake all night, reading the Bible and the Talmud. In many modern congregations, the first day of Pentecost is celebrated by the confirmation of boys and girls, a ceremony which is described in greater detail, below.

The third of the great joyous festivals is that of Tabernacles or *Sukkot,* marking the coming of the autumn and the late harvests (some time in October), and also commemorating God's protection during the period when Israel dwelt in the wilderness (Leviticus 23.43).

Both the seasonal and the historical aspects of the festival are symbolized in the *sukkah,* the booth in which observant Jews eat their meals during the holiday week. This booth is essentially a rustic cabin, with improvised walls, and a covering of leafy branches and twigs instead of a solid roof or ceiling. It is customary to adorn both the covering and the walls with vegetables and fruits, in order to make the harvest rusticity of the surroundings especially clear and emphatic.

The festival is celebrated further by the ceremonial of

the *lulab*, a cluster of a palm branch, three myrtle twigs, and two willow sprigs. During the recital of the *hallel* (i.e., Psalms 113-118) in the morning service of the festival, the *lulab* together with a citron, is taken in hand, and at certain portions of the prayer, they are moved to and fro, eastward, southward, westward, northward, upward, and downward, to indicate that God, Who is being thanked for His gifts, is to be found everywhere. At the end of the service, a scroll is taken out of the Ark, and each of those having a *lulab* marches about the scroll in a festive procession, commemorating the similar procession about the altar in Jerusalem in the days of the Temple.

On the seventh day of *Sukkot* (*Hoshanna Rabba*) there is a special service of prayer for abundant rains. After the usual service of the day, the clusters of palm branches are put down, and clusters of willow taken up (the willow symbolic of abundance of rain, because it grows by the riverside). With these willow clusters in hand, the congregation recites various hymns having the refrain *hoshanna* (or, as it was frequently pronounced in ancient times, *hosanna*) meaning, "Help, we pray Thee." At the end of these hymns, the willows are beaten against the floor of the synagogue.

Following *Hoshanna Rabba*, is the "eighth day of solemn assembly" or, as it is called in Hebrew, *Shemini Aṣeret*. This festival is intended as a climax for the joyful season, which begins with *Sukkot*. The festival is marked especially by the prayer for rain in the additional (*musaf*) service, which is therefore called *tephillat geshem* (the prayer for rain).

The final or ninth day of the autumn celebration (properly the second day of the *Shemini Aṣeret* festival) is popularly called *Simhat Torah* (the day of rejoicing in the

Law). On this day, the last section of the Five Books of Moses, *viz.*, Deuteronomy, chapter 34, as well as the first section of Genesis are read. In celebration of the annual completion and fresh beginning of the reading of the Pentateuch, all the scrolls of the Law are taken from the Ark and carried about the synagogue in a procession. To enable every member of the congregation to participate in this ceremonial, the procession moves about the synagogue hall at least seven times in the evening, and then seven times more at the morning service. It is also customary in certain rituals for each member of the congregation to participate in the public reading of the Pentateuch on *Simhat Torah*. Immediately before the reading of the last section of the Pentateuch, it is customary in most congregations to call to read from the Torah one of the distinguished members of the congregation together "with all the children" (Hebrew, *kol ha-nearim*), so that even minors may participate in the reading on this occasion.

The person called to complete the reading of the Pentateuch on *Simhat Torah* is called *hatan ha-torah* (bridegroom of the Law, popularly pronounced, *hoson torah*). The person called to read the first chapter in Genesis on that day is called *hatan bereshit* (the bridegroom of the beginning, popularly pronounced, *hoson bereshis*). These offices are usually bestowed on men of especial piety or learning, and are among the highest honors which can be given in the synagogue service.

While on these festivals communion with God is sought through joy, on *Rosh Ha-Shanah* and *Yom Kippur* it is sought through solemnity. They are described as Days of Judgment when all living things pass before God, to stand in judgment for their deeds during the past year. During the month before *Rosh Ha-Shanah* (which usually occurs during the last three weeks of September or the beginning of October), preparation is made for the festival by sounding a ram's horn at the synagogue service each morning, and reciting Psalm 27 each morning and evening. Beginning with the Sunday preceding *Rosh Ha-Shanah* (if *Rosh Ha-Shanah* occurs on Monday or Tuesday, beginning with the Sunday of the preceding week), special prayers (called *selihot*) are recited at dawn of each day, beseeching Divine forgiveness for man's transgressions. While only the most pious assemble at the synagogue to recite these prayers each day, many recite them on the first day, and on the day before *Rosh Ha-Shanah*. In some congregations, these prayers are recited at midnight rather than at dawn, to make possible a larger attendance.

The festival of *Rosh Ha-Shanah* itself is particularly devoted to prayers for peace and prosperity for all mankind, and for life and happiness for individual human beings. It also emphasizes the recognition of God as King of the universe. This phase of the festival is reflected not only in the prayers of the day, but in several of the ceremonials. The ram's horn or *shofar* is sounded before, during, and after the additional morning prayer. The notes sounded by the *shofar* tend to arouse the people to repentance, reminding them that the Kingdom of God can be realized in our hearts and in our personal lives, even in the world in which we live. In the afternoon of the first day of the festival, it is customary in many communities to walk to a river bank, as was sometimes done in ancient times at the anointing of a king. This custom of walking to the river bank is called *tashlik* (throwing), because of the popular belief that it is intended to cast off one's sins into the river.

On the evening of the first day of *Rosh Ha-Shanah*, it is

65

customary to eat apples and other fruits, dipped in honey, saying, "May it be Thy will that this year shall be happy and sweet for us." In many localities, bread is dipped in honey at all the meals eaten on *Rosh Ha-Shanah,* and during the days following it until the Day of Atonement. On the second evening of *Rosh Ha-Shanah,* it is customary to eat new fruit, over which the blessing *sheheheyanu* is recited.

The ten days beginning with the first days of *Rosh Ha-Shanah* and ending with *Yom Kippur,* are called the "Ten Days of Penitence." It is expected that everyone will observe especially high standards of ethical and ceremonial conduct during these days. There are special prayers assigned for the period, beseeching continuance of life and peace, and the *selihot* are recited on them as on the days preceding *Rosh Ha-Shanah.*

On the day preceding *Yom Kippur* (the ninth of *Tishri*) tradition prescribes festive meals. The final meal of the day, eaten before the sundown which ushers in *Yom Kippur,* thus is marked by a peculiar combination of joy and solemnity, which leaves an indelible impression. Before eating this meal, an oral confession of one's sins is recited as part of the afternoon prayer. It is also customary during the day to distribute money for charitable purposes. After the meal, the head of the household kindles a lamp or candle of sufficient size to burn for twenty-four hours, that is, until the end of the day. The mother kindles the usual festival lights, and the family proceeds to the synagogue.

The Day of Atonement is a season not only for repentance for trespasses against the ceremonial law, but more especially for trespasses committed against ethical conduct in relations between men. Forgiveness for these trespasses can only be obtained when the man who suffered wrong pardons the injustice. It is therefore customary for anyone who is conscious of having injured a neighbor, to obtain forgiveness before the Day of Atonement.

People unwittingly injure even those dear to them, including members of their families. Such thoughtlessness may raise a barrier to friendship and love. The eve of the Day of Atonement is considered an appropriate time to remove these barriers; relatives and friends call upon each other or write, offering good wishes for the coming year and either directly or indirectly asking forgiveness for any misunderstanding. Parents and grandparents bless their children and grandchildren. The moving prayer which is recited just before the evening service closes with the words: "I completely forgive anyone who has committed a trespass against me, whether against my person or against my property. . . . May no man suffer punishment because of me. And may it be Thy will, that just as I offer my forgiveness to all my fellows, that I may find grace in their eyes, so that they, too, will forgive my trespasses against them."

The Day of Atonement thus becomes a day for the renewal of bonds of affection and friendship between men.

The evening service in the synagogue, which must be recited before dark, is called *kol nidre* from its first words (meaning "all vows"). It is a service of absolution for ceremonial vows. This ceremony is made necessary by the rule of Jewish Law, requiring the fulfilment of a vow, even at great sacrifice. The vows which the ceremony of *kol nidre* releases are of course only those relating to ritual and custom. Without the consent of his neighbor, no ceremony can release anyone from a vow or promise made to his neighbor.

Because the *kol nidre* opens the service of the Day of

Atonement, it is a particularly solemn ceremony. Its melody is probably the best known of all those associated with synagogue services.

The Day of Atonement is the major fast in the Jewish calendar, a day on which all principal physical pleasures are interdicted. Men of piety also avoid wearing shoes made of leather on this day, particularly in the home or in the synagogue.[6]

The prayers of *Yom Kippur* day are so arranged that they continue uninterruptedly from their beginning in the morning until their end in the *neilah* service after sunset. At each service, there is a confession of sins and a prayer for forgiveness. During the additional prayer of the morning (*musaf*) there is a reenactment of part of the ancient service at the Temple. In the course of it, the members or at least the elders of the congregation prostrate themselves four times, just as the community gathered in the ancient Temple prostrated itself whenever the Divine Name was pronounced in the service.

The melodies of each of the *Yom Kippur* services follow definite traditions, and are reflective of the mood in which the service is expected to be pronounced. In the course of these services (as well as in those of *Rosh Ha-Shanah*) the Ark is frequently opened for the recital of especially impressive hymns and poems. The service of the Day of Atonement ends with the sounding of the ram's horn, and the joint cry by all of the congregation, "Hear, O Israel, the Lord is our God, the Lord is One."

There is a curious difference between Palestine and other countries with regard to the observance of the Jewish festivals. In Palestine Passover is observed for only

[6] Shoes or sandals were considered an object of luxury in the ancient Orient. It was therefore considered improper to wear them on days of fasting or mourning.

seven days, in accordance with the rule set down in Exodus 12.15; outside Palestine it is observed for eight days. Similarly Pentecost and *Shemini Azeret* are each observed for only one day in Palestine, but for two days outside Palestine. Moreover, in Palestine work is forbidden only on the first and seventh days of Passover, and on the first day of *Sukkot;* outside Palestine it is forbidden also on the second and on the eighth day of Passover, and on the second day of *Sukkot.*

The reason for this variation of custom is historical. In ancient times the beginning of the Jewish month was fixed when the authorities of the Temple in Jerusalem observed the new moon. As the lunar month had been accurately measured in antiquity, it was comparatively easy to foretell when the moon ought to appear in Jerusalem. But the first crescent of the new moon is frequently so thin, and sets so soon after the sun, that it was quite impossible to be certain that it had actually been observed. There was always some doubt therefore by those away from Jerusalem as to whether the Temple authorities had proclaimed one day or the next as the beginning of the calendar month.

To meet this difficulty, Temple authorities would send out messengers informing distant communities of the precise day they had fixed as new moon. These messengers were, of course, able to reach all parts of Palestine in a comparatively short time. They could not reach the distant communities of Babylonia. Hence, the Babylonian Jews were always in doubt as to whether the month had begun on the precise day of the new moon, or the day following. This put them in doubt regarding the exact day of all the festivals. Therefore, in order to avoid any possible violation of a holy day, they observed all the customs relating to each festival for an additional day. In the fifth century of the Christian era, the Jewish calendar was reduced to a fixed computative system, and thereafter no one could be in doubt with regard to the time of a festival. Nevertheless, the Jews outside of Palestine continued to observe their ancient custom. In Palestine, uncertainty regarding the precise period of the festival could occur only with regard to *Rosh Ha-Shanah,* which occurs on the first day of the month. Hence, *Rosh Ha-Shanah* is observed for two days in Palestine as well as in other countries. It is not customary to observe the Day of Atonement for two days, because it is considered impossible to impose the severity of two successive days of fasting on the whole community. Reform Jews have, in general, abandoned the observance of the second day of the holidays.

In addition to these major festivals, whose celebration is commanded in the Law of Moses, there are two lesser festivals in Judaism, which are occasions of great religious joy and sense of communion with God: *Purim,* the Feast of Esther, and *Hanukkah,* the feast signifying the rededication of the Temple during the time of the Maccabees.

In accordance with the prescription of the Book of Esther, *Purim* (occurring in the first half of March) is celebrated as a day of rejoicing and thanksgiving, with the exchange of gifts between friends, and charity to the poor. The Book of Esther is read publicly both at the evening and at the morning services. In the late afternoon, a family festival, second in importance only to that of the *seder* service, is usually held. This festive dinner is called the *seudat purim* (*Purim* meal).

Hanukkah (the midwinter festival which occurs in the

month of December) is celebrated in commemoration of the purification of the Temple by the Maccabees, after it had been defiled by the Syrian King, Antiochus IV, in the year 168 before the Christian era. Led by Judas the Maccabee, the Jews won amazing victories over outnumbering Syrian armies, and finally reconquered Jerusalem, drove the pagans out of the Temple, and reestablished it as a place for the worship of God. The day of the rededication of the Temple was the third anniversary of its first defilement, the twenty-fifth of *Kislev,* and that day, together with seven succeeding days, is observed as *Hanukkah* (the feast of dedication).

On the first night of *Hanukkah* a candle is lit, and on each succeeding night of the eight day festival, an additional candle is lit, in celebration of the holiday. It is also customary to mark the festival with family meals, games, and the exchange of gifts, particularly within the family.

Besides *Yom Kippur,* there are several lesser fasts in the Jewish calendar. Of these the most important is *Tisha B'ab* (popularly pronounced *Tishoh B'ov*), the ninth day of the month of *Ab,* the anniversary of the burning of the first and also of the second Temple. In memory of these catastrophes, it is the rule to fast from sunset on the evening before this day, until the sunset of the day itself. The Book of Lamentations is recited in the evening, and in the morning a number of dirges recording ancient and mediaeval sufferings of the Jewish people. To increase a sense of bereavement it is customary in many communities to spend the afternoon of *Tisha B'ab* visiting the graves of relatives.

There are several other fasts, less commonly observed, during which food is forbidden only during the day. These are the fast of *Gedaliah* (on the day following *Rosh*

71

Ha-Shanah); the tenth day of the month of *Tebet;* and the seventeenth day of the month of *Tammuz.* All these fasts are mentioned in Zechariah 8.19. The fast of *Gedaliah* commemorates the murder of the last governor of Judah in the year 586 before the Christian era (Jeremiah 41.2). The fast of *Tebet* commemorates the beginning of the siege of Jerusalem by the Babylonians (Ezekiel 24.1-2). The seventeenth day of *Tammuz* is the anniversary of the breach in the wall of Jerusalem by the Romans in the year 70 of the Christian era.

Partial mourning is still observed during the three weeks between the seventeenth day of *Tammuz* and the ninth of *Ab,* the period when Jerusalem was pillaged by the victorious Roman soldiery. No weddings are performed; other festivities and the wearing of new clothes are considered inappropriate. During the last nine days of this period, it is customary for many Jews to abstain from meat and wine (except on the Sabbath day).

The Jewish religious calendar begins in the autumn with *Rosh Ha-Shanah,* the festival of the New Year. The names of the months were adopted from the Babylonian calendar and are as follows: *Tishri, Marchesvan* (frequently called *Heshvan), Kislev, Tebet, Shebat, Adar, Nisan, Iyyar, Sivan, Tammuz, Ab, Ellul.*

The length of the month is fixed by the lunar cycle of twenty-nine and a half days and therefore is alternately twenty-nine and thirty days. The length of the year of twelve months is thus 354 days, though under special circumstances it may be 353 or 355 days. To make up the difference between this period and that of the solar year of 365¼ days, an additional month is added to the year, seven times in a cycle of nineteen years. This additional month is added immediately before *Nisan* (the month of the Passover) and is called the Second *Adar*. The additional month is added on the third, the sixth, the eighth, the eleventh, the fourteenth, the seventeenth, and the nineteenth years of the cycle.

Because of the character of the Jewish calendar, the beginning of each month coincides with the new moon, and the first days of the festivals of Passover and *Sukkot* (falling on the fifteenth day of their respective months) occur on the full moon.

VIII. SPECIAL OCCASIONS IN THE COURSE OF LIFE

The occasions of special joy or sadness in human life are, in Judaism, surrounded with ceremonials intended to make them means for closer communion with God. These ceremonials aid the Jew to temper joy with solemnity, and sorrow with resignation. When he is happy, the Jew is instructed to think with gratitude of God, Who is the source of happiness; and when he is in grief, he is likewise instructed to look to God, as the source of consolation. Birth, marriage, and death are thus more than incidents in temporal and sensual existence. They are occasions for thinking more deeply than usual about the meaning of existence, and the relation of man to God.

Every person born of Jewish parents (as indicated above) is considered bound to observe the covenant of Sinai, and therefore subject to the observance of Jewish ceremonial. Although mixed marriages are prohibited, the child of a Jewish mother is regarded as a Jew and needs undergo no ceremony of conversion to be admitted to the Jewish faith. A member of another faith who desires to be converted to Judaism, must (according to traditional ritual) appear before a rabbi and state his desire to be converted. The rabbi will then provide for his instruction in the elements of Jewish law, belief and practice. Before admitting him to the Jewish fold, the rabbi must warn him of the severe discipline of Judaism and the difficulties involved in adherence to the Jewish faith. If the applicant persists in his desire to enter the Jewish faith, the rabbi will arrange for the ceremony of proselytization. A male applicant must be circumcised. According to the traditional ritual followed by orthodox and conservative Jews, both male and female applicants become proselytes by immersion in a pool of running water, declaring that they are performing the ceremony in order to be admitted into the Jewish faith, and reciting as they emerge from the water the benediction, "Blessed art Thou, O Lord, our God, King of the Universe, Who didst sanctify us with Thy commandments, and hast commanded us regarding the ceremonial immersion of the proselyte." Reform rabbis do not include this ritual immersion in their ceremony of proselytization.

In accordance with the prescriptions of Genesis 17.9-14, the son of Jewish parents is circumcised on the eighth day of his life. The ceremony may be postponed for reasons of health. Because the ritual of circumcision involves at once a knowledge of surgery and of the traditional customs, it is performed by a person especially trained for the purpose, called a *mohel* (one who circumcises). At the circumcision, the father recites the benediction, "Blessed art Thou, O Lord, our God, King of the Universe, Who didst consecrate us with Thy commandments, and hast commanded us to bring this child into the covenant of our ancestor, Abraham." All those present respond, "Just as he has entered the covenant of Abraham, may he also enter into the study of the Law, into marriage, and into good deeds!" The *mohel* or some other person present, then prays for the child's future piety and welfare, and announces his name.

A girl is named at the service in the synagogue on the

Sabbath (or any other day when the Torah is read) following her birth, when the father is called to participate in the reading of the Torah. One of those present then prays for the health of the mother of the child, and for the health of the child, and announces its name.

Boys under thirteen years of age and girls under twelve years of age, are theoretically not obligated to observe the discipline of the ritual Law. In order to be trained in the Law, they are expected to observe such parts of it as they can without impairing their health. As soon as a child can speak, he is taught to recite simple evening and morning prayers, consisting primarily of the first verse of the *Shema*. When the child reaches school age, he is taught the Hebrew language, the Bible, and as he grows older, advanced Jewish studies. The instruction is given the child by his parents, by a private teacher, or in a religious school. The traditional school devoted to this purpose is called a *Talmud Torah* (the place of the study of the Law). In America, these institutions usually provide instruction for children for either three or five (in some instances, seven or ten) hours per week, after the regular secular school hours on weekdays, and on Sunday mornings. There are also Jewish day schools established in some communities, providing both secular and religious education. These are sometimes called *yeshibot* (singular, *yeshibah* or *yeshivah*, academy). The name *yeshibah* or *yeshivah* is also used for traditional schools of advanced Talmudic study in Europe, and for similar institutions in America.

A month before a boy has reached his thirteenth birthday, he is expected to begin to don the *tephillin* each morning. On the Sabbath following his thirteenth birthday, he is called to participate in the formal reading of the Torah at the usual synagogue service. The ceremony of which this is part is popularly called *bar mitzvah* (son of the commandment, in reference to his obligation to perform the commandments thereafter). Parents frequently arrange a festive celebration in honor of this occasion.

In many American synagogues similar note is taken when a girl attains the age of twelve, and therefore becomes subject to the commandments. The ceremony which is called *bat mitzvah* (daughter of the commandment, popularly pronounced *bas mitzvah*) is variously observed in different communities. In some of them, the girl is permitted to read the prophetic portion in the vernacular. In others, there is simply a family festivity.

Many conservative and reform congregations have established, either in lieu of these *bar mitzvah* and *bat mitzvah* ceremonies, or in addition to them, that of confirmation. This ritual is usually observed on Pentecost. Boys and girls of the ages of fourteen to sixteen are taught the elements of Jewish faith and history in pre-confirmation classes, and are then called to announce their devotion to the faith at a public synagogue ceremonial.

There is a considerable difference between the marriage customs of traditional and reform Jews. In the traditional service, marriages take place under a canopy (*huppah*), which symbolizes the home established through the marriage.

Judaism regards complete mutual understanding and trust between the bride and the bridegroom as a basic requirement for a valid marriage. A number of ceremonies have been established to give expression to this conception, and there are even several legal forms which emphasize it.

Before the wedding, the rabbi or other person in charge of the ceremony asks the bridegroom whether he undertakes to fulfil all the traditional obligations of a Jewish husband to his wife. These include various traditional provisions for the maintenance of the wife, both during married life, and if the occasion should arise, during her widowhood. As these are civil obligations, a formal agreement must be made to provide for them. On the bridegroom's assenting, the ceremony of *kinyan* (agreement) is performed. This consists of the rabbi handing the bridegroom an object of value, usually a handkerchief, as a symbolic consideration, to make the bridegroom's acceptance of the conditions of the marriage valid. The rabbi then draws up a document called a *ketubah* (writ, popularly pronounced *kesubah*) detailing these obligations as well as those of the wife. This *ketubah* is witnessed by two observant Jews, neither of whom may be related to the bride or bridegroom. The officiating rabbi may also act as one of these witnesses.

The language of the *ketubah* is Aramaic, the vernacular of the Jews of Palestine during the period when the present text was composed. The document is sometimes artistically decorated; and a number of the *ketubot* preserved in various museums of Jewish antiquities are of great interest to the student of art.

The wedding ceremony itself consists of a, series of benedictions, having for their purpose the expression of thanks to God for the institution of marriage and the family, for having implanted His image on the human race, and for the joy of the wedding, and including prayers for the happiness of the bride and bridegroom, and for the restoration of Jerusalem. After the first of these benedictions, the bridegroom hands the bride a ring, and says to her in Hebrew, "Thou art sanctified unto me, with this ring, in accordance with the Law of Moses and of Israel." At the end of the ceremony a glass is broken, to commemorate the destruction of Jerusalem.

In the marriage service of the reform group, the canopy and the *ketubah* are generally omitted. The wedding is usually celebrated in the synagogue. The special prayer for the restoration of Jerusalem is omitted. On the other hand, several prayers, in English, on behalf of the bride and the bridegroom, are added. The service ends with the recitation of the priestly blessing (Numbers 6.24-26) by the rabbi.[7]

Jewish Law forbids husband and wife to cohabit or to come into physical contact during the period of menstruation or for seven days afterward. At the end of the period, the wife is required to take a ritual bath in a pool of running water, or one especially built for the purpose (*mikveh*). A bride also bathes in such a *mikveh* before her wedding. The value of these regulations in preserving Jewish family life and in the prevention of certain diseases, has been recognized by various Christian and Jewish writers on genetics.[8]

In Jewish Law marriage can be terminated by a religious divorce (called *get*). In practice such a divorce is granted by a rabbi only if both parties consent, and have already been divorced in the civil courts. The ritual of divorce is extremely complicated, and is performed only by especially trained scholars. Reform rabbis generally recognize a civil divorce as terminating a Jewish marriage, from a religious as well as from the secular point of view,

[7] *Rabbi's Manual*, edited and published by the Central Conference of American Rabbis, Cincinnati, 1928, p. 39, ff.
[8] For a further discussion and bibliography, see Mrs. R. L. Jung, in *The Jewish Library*, edited by Rabbi Leo Jung, Third Series, pp. 355-365.

and therefore do not insist on a religious divorce as pre-requisite for remarriage of either husband or wife.

There is one instance in traditional Jewish Law in which the death of the husband does not completely break the marriage bond; that is the case of a childless widow, described in Deuteronomy 25.5-10. Biblical Law, as stated in Deuteronomy, requires such a childless widow to marry her husband's brother, so that her first-born son, by the second marriage, may "succeed in the name of the brother which is dead, that his name be not put out of Israel." Later rabbinic ordinances forbade the performance of such a Levirate marriage, but nevertheless insisted that the widow may not remarry without performing the ceremony of *halitzah*, ordained in Deuteronomy, as alternative to such a marriage.

When a Jew feels that his end is approaching, he should confess his sins in accordance with the fixed ritual, making special mention, however, of any sin which he is conscious of having committed, and which is not mentioned in the traditional formula. In his last conscious moments, he recites the traditional confession of faith, "Hear, O Israel, the Lord is our God, the Lord is One." Those about him may help him recite the formula, by repeating it with him.

According to rabbinic tradition, the body should be washed after death and dressed in linen shrouds. The universal use of linen shrouds dates back to the beginning of the second century of the Christian era. Rabban Gamaliel II, the head of the Academy of Jabneh and one of the most distinguished scholars and communal leaders of his time, specifically requested that no elaborate provision such as was then customary be made for his burial, but that he be interred in a shroud like those used for the poor. The custom has been universally adopted by observant Jews to stress further the equality of all men.

The body must be interred in the ground, as soon after death as possible. Cremation is forbidden, as being an implicit denial of the resurrection.

The funeral service is usually recited in the home of the deceased, though in the case of a person of especial piety, it may be recited in the synagogue. Because of the conditions of modern urban life, funeral services are sometimes held in rooms especially devoted to that purpose, so-called funeral chapels. The purpose of the service and the ceremonies associated with it, is to give expression to the natural grief of the bereaved, and at the same time to inculcate in the bereaved resignation to the will of God.

The service consists of the recital of one or more psalms and selections of appropriate verses from other psalms. Usually Psalm 16, 23, 90, or 91 is recited. The reading of the psalm may be followed by an address; and the service closes with a prayer for the peace of the soul of the deceased. This prayer is repeated at the grave, and a second psalm is recited, after which the bereaved recite the *kaddish*. Either during the funeral services or immediately before the burial, the person officiating at the ceremonies asks the near relatives of the deceased (husband, wife, son, daughter, father, mother, brother, or sister) to cut one of their garments. This ceremony is called *keriah* (tearing the garment) and is reminiscent of the ancient Jewish usage of tearing one's clothes in bereavement (see II Samuel 1.11). After tearing the garment, each of the bereaved recites the blessing of resignation to the justice of God: "Blessed art Thou, O Lord, our God, King of the Universe, the true Judge."

During the week after the burial of a relative, near

81

relatives, including husband, wife, children, brothers, sisters, and parents, remain at home. They must not engage in any gainful occupation, unless the income is vital to their subsistence, or unless they will forfeit their employment. It is customary for friends to visit the mourners to console them, and to arrange public prayers in the house of the deceased. During the whole week of mourning (called *shiva*, seven, i.e., the seven days of mourning) a lamp is kept burning in the house of the deceased. None of the mourners wears any jewels, and mirrors, considered a luxury, are covered. The mourners sit on low stools, instead of chairs; they do not study the Law or the Scriptures, save such solemn works as the Books of Job and Lamentations, the dire prophecies in Jeremiah, and the laws of mourning in the Talmud and Codes; and they are forbidden to wear shoes made of leather.

After the completion of the *shiva*, the relatives observe partial mourning for the remainder of the month. They do not don new clothes, and avoid taking part in festivities, or listening to music. On the death of a parent, this partial mourning is observed for a whole year. In order to make grief itself a means for closer communion with God, the child is expected, during this year of mourning, to be particularly mindful of religious observances, to attend synagogue service regularly, and to recite the *kaddish* at each prayer. Whenever possible, the bereaved son serves as reader of the public prayers on weekdays during this year of mourning. These customs are also observed on the anniversary of the death of one's parents. Such an anniversary is called *yahrzeit* (a German name, because the custom assumed its present form among the German Jews). It is customary, also, to have a light burning at home during the day marking the anniversary of the death of a near relative. This light symbolizes the belief in human immortality, in accordance with the rabbinic interpretation of the verse (Proverbs 20.27), "The spirit of man is the lamp of God, searching all the inward parts." About a year after the death of a relative, the mourners set up a monument marking the place of the grave. At the unveiling of this monument, called *maṣṣebah* (pillar, popularly pronounced *matzevah*), psalms are read, prayers are recited for the peace of the soul of the deceased, and the *kaddish* is repeated.

IX. THE JEWISH HOME AND THE DIETARY LAWS

Like every other authentic experience, training, or ambition, piety cannot stop short of the home. If religion were to be merely ecclesiastical, it would soon cease to be that, too. The psalmist who was told "Let us go up to the house of the Lord," rejoiced because in his own house the reality of God was never forgotten. Throughout Jewish history indeed the attempt to reproduce in the home the order and mood of the place of worship has never been relaxed.

The interrelationship of sanctuary and home has been responsible for at least two significant results. On the one hand, the Jew did not remain a stranger to the ceremonial and purpose of his sacred institutions. On the other hand, his home and home life were transfigured. His residence became a habitation of God. What might have been nothing more than a functional shelter acquired a surplus value.

This sanctification of the home was achieved by a religious discipline whose purpose was constantly to prompt a remembrance of God. The Jew who visited the ancient Temple, for example, readily understood that the elaborate rites, precautions, exactitudes, purifications, were the appropriate expressions of the beauty of holiness. "If you were to serve a king of flesh and blood," the saintly Hillel once reminded a guest, "would you not have to learn how to make your entrances and exits and obeisances?

How much more so in the service of the King of kings of kings!"

That such fastidiousness was therefore required in God's House the Jew accepted as unquestioningly as we accept beautiful form on occasions of state or solemnity. The forms reminded him of God. And because they did, and because Israel's teachers tried to prevent the Jew from forgetting God even when he was away from the Sanctuary, corresponding rituals and attitudes were introduced into the Jewish home. Thus the Jewish home became a sanctuary in miniature, its table an altar, its furnishings instruments for sanctity.

In a sense, every detail of home life is an expression of the pattern of sanctity. Jewish homes, for example, are generally expected to contain the basic religious texts like the Bible, usually accompanied at least with the commentary of Rashi, the Talmud, perhaps an abbreviated code (the short Shulhan Aruk), some of the magnificent moralistic works, and of course the Prayer Book—which is actually one of the most extraordinary anthologies of Jewish classical literature. It is not uncommon to find in a traditional Jewish home an excellent library with volumes which have been handed down from father to son, volumes which reveal constant use. Just as we might say that no cultured home lacks its Shakespeare volumes, its classics, its pictures, so the Jew would say that no home, since it is a field for holiness, can be fully furnished without the literature which teaches man about God.

Similarly, the various family festival celebrations with their rituals (see above chapter VII) constitute activities which bring the divine message very close to the Jew. It is an insensitive Jewish child indeed who forgets the beauty of the Seder at Passover, or the kindling of the lights during Hanukkah, or the sight of his mother kindling the Sabbath lamps at dusk. These and like activities collaborate to make holiness a familiar emphasis and delight.

Part of the daily pattern of sanctity is formed by the so called dietary laws. As is well known, Jewish law prohibits the eating of certain foods. These prohibitions are enumerated essentially in Leviticus, chapter 11, and again in Deuteronomy, chapter 14. No vegetable growths are prohibited; but of animal life the Law permits fish which have scales and fins, certain types of fowl, and only those quadrupeds which chew their cud and have cloven hoofs. Among the domestic quadrupeds this includes only oxen, sheep, and goats.

According to traditional Judaism, warm blooded animals may be eaten only if they are ritually slaughtered, i.e., if they are slaughtered in the manner used in the Temple for sacrificial purposes. The knife used in slaughtering must be sharp, and must be examined both before and after slaughtering, to be certain that its edge contains no notch, which by tearing the animal's throat might give it unnecessary pain. The animal must not, however, be stunned before slaughtering, for stunning prevents the free flow of the blood, and the absorption of the blood in the meat makes the food prohibited. To insure the animal's speedy death, the person who slays it must be trained for the work. He must be capable of examining the knife to be sure that it contains no notch; he must know enough of the diseases of animals to be able to examine the body, and to make certain that it was suffering from no serious disease. A person so trained is called a *shohet* (slaughterer). In order to be allowed to perform his duties, he must receive authorization from a rabbi.

After an animal is slaughtered, its lungs are examined to guard against symptoms of various communicable diseases, mainly tuberculosis. The Talmud, its commentaries, and the later codes, contain an impressive amount of veterinary information regarding the symptoms of disease in animals, so that an examination based on this information is a means of detecting disease.

If an animal has been found to be free from serious disease, its meat is declared *kasher* (fit, popularly pronounced *kosher*).

The meat must not, however, remain unwashed for three days. If it does, the surface blood is believed to be absorbed in the tissues; and the food becomes prohibited. After the meat is cut, the various parts are placed in a container of water for half an hour to be cleansed of such surface blood as adheres to them. Thereafter the meat is covered with salt, further to draw out the blood, and remains in the salt for at least an hour. The salt is then washed off, and the meat may be boiled. Meat which is to be roasted on a spit need not be soaked in water or salted. Meat from the udder or the liver may be prepared only by roasting.

In addition to the various laws prohibiting certain types of food, there is a rule mentioned thrice in the Scripture against seething a kid in its mother's milk (Exodus 23.19; 34.26; and Deuteronomy 14.21). This rule was originally intended, according to Maimonides, to extirpate an idolatrous practice. It is interpreted as prohibiting the cooking or eating the meat of any warm blooded animal with milk, or a derivative of milk. Hence, it is prohibited to serve meat and milk or butter or cheese at the same meal. In order to avoid any possibility of a mixture of meat and milk, observant Jews provide themselves with two types of dishes, one of which is used only for meat foods, the other only for milk foods. Further, it is customary in many countries not to eat milk dishes for six hours after a meat meal.

Scripture is quite brief in outlining the regulations governing diet, so that the various theories about the dietary laws remain in the last analysis purely speculative. Why certain animals should have been permitted and why others should have been forbidden as food we do not know. But the purpose for these regulations is explicitly stated (see Leviticus 11:45): "Be ye therefore holy, for I (the Lord) am holy."

X. THE JEWISH HOPE FOR THE FUTURE

Virtually every prophet in Scripture has predicted that in the fulness of time, man will gain a more complete understanding of God, and will inaugurate a reign of justice and peace on earth. According to the interpretation of this prophecy in the Talmud and later writers, this age of universal peace will be established by a great, but humble teacher of the lineage of David: the Messiah. Reform and many conservative Jews, on the other hand, expect that the Messianic age will come about through the gradual enlightenment of men, and through the work of many thinkers and teachers. All agree that the age will be one of profound and universal faith in God, recognition of human brotherhood, and an unprecedented knowledge of the universe. There will be no discrimination between persons because of sex, origin, faith, occupation, nationality, or any other reason. The evils of human origin will have been overcome; those inherent in Nature will be mitigated through further knowledge and increased piety. In this world of brotherly love, there will be no room for pride in achievement, nor for memories of past bitterness and oppression.

The prophetic tradition, originating in the teachings of Moses, may be considered a continuous endeavor, looking to the fulfilment of this vision. Together with other faiths derived from Scripture, Judaism has a unique contribution to make to the enlightenment of the world. Its special contribution consists, in part, in the preservation of the Hebrew language, and the original form of the Hebrew Scriptures, as well as in the transmission unchanged of the ethical, ceremonial, and intellectual discipline which were native to the Prophets and the later sages.

The increase of hatred and persecution in our day does not weaken the Jew's faith in God and in His prophets or his conviction that ultimately the age of universal human brotherhood will be established on earth. In the most trying moments of his own and world history, the Jew repeats, with assurance, the ancient declaration, "Thou art faithful, O Lord, our God, and Thy words are faithful. And not one word of Thine shall ultimately remain unfulfilled; for Thou art a great, holy, Divine King."

INDEX

Aaron, 44
Abraham, 39
Akiba, Rabbi, 61
Albo, Joseph, 26, 27
'Amidah, 43-5
Amos, 24
Antigonus of Socho, 25
Antiochus IV, 71
Aramaic, 48, 78
Ark, in synagogue, 10
  scroll in, 10, 40
Atonement, Day of, 19, 43, 66
Authority, central of Jewish people, 12

Babylonia, 8
Bahya Ibn Pakuda, 18
Balfour Declaration, 34
Bar mitzvah, 77
Bat mitzvah, 77
Ben Azzai, 24
Bialik, Chayyim Nahman, 53
Bible, 1, 4, 5, 40, 48, 62, 76, 85, 86-7
  See under individual books; also
    Scroll, Scriptures, Pentateuch
Blessings, 4, 36-8, 52-3, 79
Duties of the Heart, Book of, 18

Calendar, Jewish religious, 72-3
Caro, Rabbi Joseph, 17
Central Conference of American
  Rabbis, platform of, 27
Charity, 17, 30, 66
Child, Jewish, admission to faith, 5
  education of, 12, 75
  and seder, 60
  and Simhat Torah, 64
Chofetz Chayyim, 18
Chosen People, The, Meaning of
  the Concept, 25
Christianity, 6, 32
Circumcision, 74-5

Citizenship, 29
Columbus Platform, 27
Commandments
  Revelation of, 5
  Ten, 10, 40-1
  festival of, 62
Community, prayers for, 45
Conduct, ethical, 17, 66
Conduct, moral, among Jews, 7
  and neighbors, 19
Confirmation, 62, 77
Conservative Judaism, 14
Conversion, 5; 6; n., 14; 74
Courtesy, 3
Covenant, between God and Moses
  on Mt. Sinai, 4, 14, 74
Creed, Jewish, 26
Cremation, 81
Crescas, Hasdai, 26
Crusades, 8

Daily services, 46
Deuteronomy, 48, 57, 64, 79-80,
  86, 87
Dietary Laws, 83-5
Discipline, of Judaism, 8
Diseases, prevention of, 79
  detecting of, 84
Divorce, 79

Elijah, 60
Emden, Rabbi Jacob, 32; n., 33
Esther, Book of, 5, 70
Ethics, place in Judaism, 7, 15, 18,
  19, 30
Exodus, Book of, 48, 62, 84
Ezekiel, 72
Ezra, 4

Faith, respect for religious, 16
Family, 6, 31, 70, 77, 78-9
Fasman, Oscar Z., n., 33
Fast, 68, 71

Festivals, 31, 50-73, 56
Forgiveness, 22, 66
Friendship, 3, 23, 67
Funeral services, 80

Gamaliel II, Rabban, 44, 80
Gedaliah, 71-2
Gehenna, 24
Genesis, Book of, 39, 64, 75
Get (writ of divorcement), 79
God, 4, 28, 30
    communion with, 3, 10, 13, 24,
      31, 36, 50, 53, 55, 64, 81, 82
    kingdom of, 3, 29, 46, 61, 65
    fatherhood of, 8
    will of, 8, 81
    recognition of, 16
    love of for man, 22
    return to, 22
    man created in Image of, 23, 24
    presence of, 50
    understanding of, 86
    faith in, 86-87
Government, civil, 7, 8, 15; prayers
    for, 8; and justice, 30

Habdalah, 54
Haftarah, 46
Haggadah. See Passover *Haggadah*
Hagiographa, the, 4
Halitzah, 80
Hallah, 52
Hallel, 63
Haninah, Rabbi, 8
Hannah, 39
Hanukkah, 70, 86
Hatan bereshit, 64
Hatan ha-torah, 64
Hazzan, 42
Hebrew, language, 11, 31, 34, 48,
    76, 86
Hebrew Theological College, 13
Hebrew Union College, 13
Hebrew University, 34
Hillel, 84
Hillul ha-Shem, 15-16
Holy Days. See festivals
Home, Jewish. See family
Hoshanna Rabba, 63
Hoshen Mishpat, 17
Huppah, 77

Immersion. See conversion
Immortality, 24, 28
Injustice, victim of, 19

Interment, 80
Isaacs, Prof. Nathan, n., 10
Islam, 6, 31
Israel. See Columbus Platform

Jacob, 39
Jacob, Rabbi, 19
Jeremiah, 72
Jerusalem, Temple of, 8, 10, 39.
    41, 68, 71, 83
    prayer for welfare of, 33
    siege of, 72
    restoration of, 78
    destruction of, 12, 78
Jewish Institute of Religion, 13
Jewish Theological Seminary of
    America, 13
Jews, orthodox, 27
    conservative, 27, 86
    reform, 27, 86
    Ashkenazic, Saphardic, 58
    See also *Judaism*
Josephus, 7
Judaism, definition of, 3
    apostasy from, 14
    rabbinic, 25
    foundations of, 28
    way of life, 31
    interpretations of. See Conserva-
      tive, Orthodox, and Reform
      Judaism
Judas the Maccabee, 71
Judgment, Days of, 64
Jung, Rabbi Leo, n., 10; n., 83
Justice, 3, 86
    Jewish conception of, 17
    social, 30

Kaddish, 45, 81-2
Kahan, Rabbi Israel Meir, 18
Kasher, 87
Keriah, 81
Ketubah, 78
Kiddush, 52
Kiddush ha-Shem, 15
Kinyan, 77
Kittel, 60
Kol ha-nearim, 64
Kol nidre, 67
Kosher. See *kasher*

Lag Ba'Omer, 61
Lamentations, Book of, 71
Languages, Semitic, 11

Law, Biblical, 9, 14
  ceremonial, 3, 7, 66
  civil, 16, 17, 34
  interpretation of, 12
  study of, 12
  Talmudic, 10, 14, 16
  teaching of, 10
Laws, Dietary, 83-5
Levites, 44
Leviticus, 19, 62, 86, 88
Liberty, human, 57
Lights, Sabbath, 51-2
  festival, 66
  Hanukkah, 71
  on anniversary of death of relative, 82
Liturgy, 26
Love, of God, 30
  of fellow-man, brotherly, 86
Lulab, 63

Ma'arib, 43
Maccabees, 70-1
Maftir, 46
Maimonides, 24, 26, 33, 48, 84
Malachi, 61
Man, dignity and worth of, as a child of God, 8
Marriage, 6, 47, 74, 77-8
Martyrdom, 15
Massah, 57
Massebalo, 82
Matzah. See *Massah*
Matzah meal, 58
Matzevah. See *massebah*
Meal, Sabbath, 52-3
Melodies, 68
Messiah, the, 89
Mezuman, 37
Mezuzot, 49
Mikveh, 79
Minhah, 43
Minyan, 42
Mixed Marriage, child of, 6, 74
Mizrachi, 35
Mohammedanism. See Islam
Mohel, 75
Monotheism, Jewish attitude to, 6
Months, length of, 72
Moses, Five Books of, 4, 10, 11, 46, 64
Moses, teachings of, 5, 89
Mourning, 72
Musaf, 43, 44, 56, 66, 68

Naming of children, 75
Nehemiah, 4, 5
Ne'ilah, 43, 68
New Year's Day. See *Rosh Ha-Shanah*
Numbers, Book of, 44, 79

Oneg shabbat, 54
Orthodox Judaism, 14

Paganism, 7, 29
Palestine, Talmud of, 8
  rehabilitation of, 29, 33-4
  welfare of, 33
  educational system, 34
  mandate for, 34
  return to, 39
  festivals in, 68-9
Parents, Jewish, obligation of, 5
  to teach, 12, 76
Passover Haggadah, 60
Passover services, 50, 52, 55, 59, 56-61, 73
Patriotism, 8
Peace, 30, 86
Pentateuch, 46, 64
  See also under individual books and Moses, Five Books of
Pentecost. See *Shabuot*
Pesach. See Passover
Philanthropy, 3, 17
  See also Charity
Philo, 7
Polytheism, 7
Practice, religious, 31
Prayer, 3, 10, 31, 39-49, 65-6, 68, 78, 81
Prayers, for government, 7-8
Prophets, the, 4, 8, 39, 46
  See also individual names
Proselyte, 5
Proselytization. See conversion
Proverbs, Book of, 82
Psalms, Book of, 63
Punishment, 24
Purim, 70

Rabbi Isaac Elchanan Theological Seminary, 13
Rabbis, 13, 14, 42, 53, 74, 77
Reform Judaism, 14
Repentance, 22-3, 66
Resurrection, 80
Revelation, the, 5, 14, 25, 62

INDEX

Rosh Ha-Shanah, 50, 64-6
Rules of conduct, 3, 8

Sabbath, the, 19, 31, 50-73
  lights (See lights) services, 52-3
Sacrifices, 8
Salanter, Rabbi Israel, 19
Sanhedrin, 12
School, Jewish, 31, 76
Schools, ancient Babylonian and
    Palestinian, 8, 12
  American rabbinical, 13
Scriptures, cantillation of, 42
Scriptures, study of, 8, 34
Scroll, preparation of, 11
Scroll, sacredness, 10
Scroll, text of, 11
Sedakah. See charity
Seder, 59
Selihot, 65, 66
Seudah shelishit, 53
Seudat purim, 70
Shabuot, 50, 55, 61-2, 77
Shaharit, 43
Shalosh Seudot. See *Seudah Sheli-shit*
Shammash, 43
Sheheheyanu, 52, 66
Shema, 45, 76
Shemini Aseret, 63
Shemoneh 'esreh, 44
Shield of David, 41
Shiva, 81-2
Shofar, 65
Shohet, 86
Shulhan Aruk, 17, 85
Simhat Torah, 63
Sins, Confession of, 19, 80
Sisit, 48
Sofer, definition of, 11
Solomon, 39
Study, purpose of, 4, 12; of Scrip-
    tures, 8; duty of, 10-14, 76

Sukkah, 62
Sukkot, 50, 55, 62, 73
Synagogue, 6, 31, 66
  Scroll in, 10
  and prayers, 39-49
  architecture of, 40
  American, 40-1

Tabernacles. See *Sukkot*
Tallit, 48
Talmud, 9, 12, 24, 34, 61, 62, 89
Talmud Torah, 76
Tashlik, 65
Teachers, 4, 86
Teaching, 10
Temple. See Jerusalem, Temple of
Ten Days of Penitence, 66
Tephillat geshem, 63
Tephillin, 4, 48, 76
Tisha B'ab, 71
Torah, 4, 23, 28, 46-7
  See also Pentateuch; Moses, Five
    Books of
Tradition, Jewish, 4
  prophetic, 86
Traditions, oral, 9
Transgression, 22-3

Universal brotherhood, age of, 87

Vengeance, prohibition of, 18
Vows, 67

Wedding, 61, 72, 78
Widow, 79

Yahrzeit, 82
Yeshibot, 76
Yigdal, 26
Yohai, Rabbi Simeon ben, 61
Yom Kippur, 50, 64, 66-8

Zionists, 35
Zizith. See *Sisit*

CPSIA information can be obtained
at www.ICGtesting.com
Printed in the USA
BVHW041607101220
595274BV00025B/1535